THE ULTIMATE

Key West

TRAVEL GUIDE

VOLUME 2

MARK LEE

CONTENTS

Looking south to Cuba. The Southernmost Point, iconic landmark and symbol of Key West, can be found at the corner of South and Whitehead Streets. Get there early as I did this November morning to get the best shots without standing in line with the crowds of tourists. Photo by Mark Lee

INTRODUCTION

Thanks for reading the *Ultimate Key West Travel Guide*. I hope that my book gets you started on a great adventure to Key West and The Florida Keys. When my wife and I first went to the Florida Keys in the late 1990s we couldn't believe our eyes as we drove down the Overseas Highway. It was literally like driving to another country because it was so different from any of the coastlines we had seen before on our travels.

We thought that you had to go to the Bahamas to see such clear green water or the South Pacific islands to see such sweeping, breathtaking vistas of swaying coconut palms set against a brilliant blue sky. Since then we have returned time after time and go back to many of our tried and true favorites, but also try to experience some of the new places that have opened since our last visit. We've made some really good friends in our travels and have found the people of Key West to be some of the warmest, most inviting folks that you will ever meet. Key West is such a special seaside community to us and we want to share some of our favorite places to go and things to do..

So many times when I talk to people about Key West, the main impression that they have is only about the bar scene up and down Duval Street. Although many of my favorite haunts are on Duval or close by, this town has so much more to offer than just bars. What we have found is that when you wander away from Duval, off the beaten path, you meet the real Key West and experience a different side of the island.

There is so much history associated with this mysterious island and much of that is captured in its top rated museums such as the ones that the Key West Art and Historical Society maintain. Certainly Key West's story could not be told without including the Shipwreck Museum due the integral part that the wrecking and salvage industry played in its development. It was also this same industry that made it at one time the wealthiest town in the United States. One of its larger than life former residents, Mel Fisher, is highlighted in the museum that carries his name, the Mel Fisher Maritime Museum. A must see is the exhibit that highlights the diminutive Key Wester known as Robert the Doll.

Key West has great restaurants, wonderful scenery, and great music. It has seafood so fresh that what you dine on in the evening was probably swimming in the ocean just that morning. Some of the most talented and dedicated charter boat captains around are waiting to take you on an offshore adventure whether its big game fish that you seek or sightseeing in some of its remote areas for wildlife beauty. You'll find nightly entertainment at Mallory Square at the longstanding tradition, the Sunset Celebration. There are tall ships, sleek catamarans, or intimate smaller sailboats available to take you on a memorable sunset cruise around Key West. A multitude of adventures await you, just pick one and go. You'll read about many of these opportunities that await you in my book and more. So if you're ready let's shove off and let the adventures begin.

AND FIRST A LITTLE HISTORY

People have been coming to Key West since before recorded time. I guess generally speaking they were looking for some of the same things that we look for today. The Native Americans came to Key West for the food and water. Today's tourists are still looking for food, but they find their "water" at Sloppy Joes in the form of beer and Sloppy Ritas. The rocky shores of the Florida Keys were first traversed by the Native American Indian tribes who called this area home. Legend has it that the Calusa Indians inhabited these islands and engaged in a fierce battle with another of the indigenous tribes of Florida. After this bloody battle the island was strewn with the bodies of fallen warriors and their skeletons were left to bleach in the sun. Years later when Spanish explorers happened upon the ghastly sight of all of those bones it they called it Cayo Hueso or Bone Island. The discoverer Hernando Desoto came to Key West on behalf of Spain in 1521. In 1815 Don Juan de Estrada, the Spanish governor of Florida, granted claim to Key West to Juan de Salas for his service to his country. Juan, a true capitalist at heart and by all tales the perpetrator of the first real estate scam in the state of Florida, sold his interest in Key West to two different gentlemen without their knowledge. He first sold it to John Strong who in turn sold to John Geddes of Charleston. De Salas also sold the same property to John Simonton, a well to do businessman from Mobile Alabama. Simonton's friend and associate John Whitehead had previously seen Key West and its clear waters teaming with turtle and fish. He had made note of its strategic location and proximity to the shipping routes which ran from New York to the Gulf of Mexico and its ports in Mobile and New Orleans. It could also be an important waypoint for ships steaming from the Gulf to Cuba and points southward. Simonton and Whitehead also had two other partners in their endeavor, Pardon Green and John Fleeming. As

Simonton became aware of the other claims to this time share gone wild in the making he used his influence and government connections in Washington to secure his claim on his purchase. In the end, the US Land Claim board ratified his claim on Key West. As you drive the around town you'll see street signs that bear witness to his presence by using his name as well as his partners'.

With all of that behind them there was still the specter of piracy that pervaded the Keys and the rest of the Caribbean. Blackbeard the Pirate, yes The Blackbeard, had established Key West as his base and set about increasing his fortunes at the expense of the rest of the world's shipping interests. Not only that, but any number of privateers also sailed with the sponsorship of foreign countries preying on ships at sea and loading their coffers up all the while lining their own pockets with the riches of the New World. To quell all of this maritime mayhem, Commodore David Porter was sent to Key West to establish a base of operation and stop the raids on shipping in the West Indies. Porter was so good at this job that within a year he had pretty much eradicated the Caribbean of the threat of piracy.

With the threat of pirates absent from the seas, another maritime industry called wrecking started to grow in importance on the island. The word "wrecking" refers to the rescuing of crews and passengers and the salvage and transport of cargo to shore. When ships would become snarled on a coral reef out in the waters of Key West, word would ring out throughout the town and the race would be on. The first party to make it out to the ship would make claim and rescue the crew as well as salvage the cargo. For their daring efforts, the wreckers were well compensated. Also, laws had been passed by Congress that stated that salvaged goods would have to be brought to a US port of entry. This kept the cargo from going to a foreign port and thus losing income. These goods were brought to port to be warehoused and later sold which helped to increase the wealth of the wreckers in Key West. With the appearance of lighthouses in the Keys and better navigational aids and charts the wrecking industry declined due to lack of supply.

In the late 1840s the sponging industry started to take off. Due to the quality and variety of product available, the Key West sponge

THE ULTIMATE KEY WEST TRAVEL GUIDE

proved to be very popular. The sponge fishermen would go out in small boats called "hook boats." Once over the sponge beds they would use long poles with three and four pronged rakes to harvest the sponges from the ocean floor. In its heyday, the sponging industry brought in an average of 2000 tons per year with a value of $750,000 to the local economy. The first sponge docks were located where the Conch Republic Restaurant and A & B Lobster House sit today. In the end, overfishing and a deadly fungus led to the demise of this industry.

Cigar manufacturing played a large role in the island economy of Key West. The first cigar factory opened in Key West around 1831, but the industry did not flourish until after the U.S. Civil War. During the years of 1868-1878 there was a large influx of Cubans who immigrated to Key West. This period in Cuban history is known as the Ten Years War and was part of Cuba's fight for independence from Spain. Most of the immigrants that came to Key West during this time were of middle and working-class backgrounds. These Cuban exiles brought with them a strong work ethic and the art of cigar making.

By the mid-1870s no fewer than 29 cigar factories were in operation turning out more than 60 million cigars per year. By the 1890s over 100 million cigars per year were being produced in Key West. One of the most influential of the cigar factory proprietors was Eduardo Gato who was the first Cuban to own a major Key West cigar factory. He not only built and operated the factory, but also had cottages constructed to house his workers. His former factory building still stands today at 1100 Simonton Street and serves as government offices for Monroe County. The Great Fire of 1886 destroyed 11 of the cigar factories and was the beginning of the end of this industry in the Keys. Although factories were rebuilt and reopened it was labor unrest and the organization of unions that led to the relocation of most of this industry out of town. By 1931 all of the major cigar factories had closed, many of whom moved to the Tampa area.

With Key West being the last island in the chain of the Florida Keys it was also the least accessible and could only be reached by water. This would all change due to the dream and extraordinary efforts of millionaire Henry Morrison Flagler. Flagler was a cofounder and partner with

John D. Rockefeller in the Standard Oil Company. Flagler and his wife moved to Florida after she was diagnosed with tuberculosis. Her physician had suggested that she seek a warmer alternative to the cold snowy winters of New York. They settled in Jacksonville, but her health rapidly declined and they summarily moved back to New York after a short time in Florida. After his wife's death, Flagler remarried and went to St. Augustine where he reduced his work load and transitioned to a new career, railroad building. He started by buying the short line Jacksonville, St. Augustine, and Halifax River Railway. This would guarantee delivery of material and supplies to St. Augustine where he was building three new hotels. Flagler had also begun a foray into hotel building due to his dissatisfaction with the facilities that he found when he traveled to the Sunshine State. In fact, as he began his march down the East coast of Florida with his railroads he built major hotel facilities and the infrastructure to support them. He extended his railroad holdings farther down the coast to Ormond Beach and then on to Palm Beach. In Palm Beach he built two hotels, one of which would become The Breakers. He found that even Palm Beach was susceptible to the cold with the great freezes of 1894 and 1895. He discussed this with Julia Tuttle, known as the "Mother of Miami," who suggested he move to south of Fort Lauderdale which was untouched by freezes. In Flagler's mind, his goal was to be in Key Biscayne, but this was a move that he was not fully prepared to make yet. However, a generous land grant agreement with the Florida legislature whereby he was granted 8000 acres for every mile of track laid helped to change his mind. It also did not hurt that the Brickell and Tuttle families contributed a combined 600 acres to Flagler to further entice him. This prime acreage skirted both sides of the Miami River and would become the downtown Miami of today. In 1902 he authorized a survey of the best route to Key West and in 1905 it was announced to the public that the Florida East Coast Railway would extend its southern line all the way to Key West.

At a cost of 50 million dollars, the Overseas Railway was constructed through some of the harshest conditions imaginable through the Everglades, mangroves, and across the emerald waters of the Florida Keys. A total workforce of over 40,000 would be used during its construction with no more than 5000 working at any given time. On January 22 the first passenger train arrived in Key West with Flagler and his wife on board a luxurious special Pullman car. A special ceremony was held to commemorate the event with speeches by President Taft and Flagler. With the arrival of the railroad, Key West was now connected to the rest of the world by rail transportation as well as mail, telegraph, and telephone.

The railroad continued to operate until the Great Labor Day Hurricane of 1935. This massive storm devastated the Upper and Middle Keys causing much death and destruction. Many sections of the railway roadbed were damaged and would be very costly to repair. However, the bridges remained intact and could be reused. As you travel down highway US 1 through the Florida Keys you can see the remnants of the once great Overseas Railway. The bridges and viaducts still stand in the water where they were built more than 100 years ago and once supported the tracks that ran to Key West from the mainland. After the demise of the railroad, the old roadbed and bridges were used as the basis for the Overseas Highway that automobiles would use to drive to Key West. In 1982 thirty seven of the original bridges were replaced by the wider more modern versions on which we ride today.

Key West

DRINKS AND FOOD

SLOPPY JOE'S

201 Duval Street

(305) 294-5717

Monday thru Saturday 9:00 a.m. – 4:00 a.m.

Sunday 12:00 p.m. – 4:00 a.m.

www.sloppyjoes.com

Located at the corner of Duval and Greene Streets since 1937, Sloppy Joe's has been at the top of the list in Key West bar lore. The official opening of Sloppy Joe's came with the repeal of prohibition on December 5, 1933, a short distance down Greene Street, which paved the way for Joe "Josie" Russell to open his first legitimate bar under the name of the Blind Pig.

Previously, Russell had been one of a group of Key West entrepreneurs who operated illegal speakeasies. A short time later, the bar changed names and became the Silver Slipper with the addition of a dance floor. It was with the third and final name change that the bar became Sloppy Joe's as we know it today. This name was chosen at the suggestion of a good friend and most favored patron, Ernest Hemingway. It was so named in honor of one of Ole Hem's favorite bars in Havana, Cuba, which was owned by Jose Garcia. Hemingway was a good friend and fishing buddy of Josie Russell and a daily customer of the bar. Every afternoon after he had spent his morning writing, he would walk down to Sloppy Joe's, that is if he wasn't out on another offshore fishing adventure with the proprietor.

Originally located a short walk down Greene Street, it moved from its location due to the "outrageous" rent increase of one dollar per week. Legend has it that the bar never really closed. Around midnight, the bar patrons simply picked up their drinks and all of the furniture in the bar and moved down to 201 Duval Street where service resumed without interruption.

Today, Sloppy Joe's is a legendary destination that everyone seeks out upon arriving in Key West. Big things happen at Sloppy Joes from its commanding position at the corner of Duval and Greene Streets.

11

Kenny Chesney chose to host his Kenny in the Keys event in March 2016, which was a small "warm up concert," at Sloppy Joes. It was a chance to practice the music for the upcoming tour and have a good time doing it in one of his favorite places. Due to the popularity of both Chesney and Sloppy Joe's, fans could be seen camping out on the sidewalk well before dawn. As the doors closed on the bar at 4 am, the faithful could be seen lining up on the sidewalk to get a spot inside for that night's show.

The ever popular Hemingway Days Festival was spawned at Sloppy Joe's in 1981. This yearly celebration is held the 3rd week of July and centered around the birthday of Ernest Hemingway which is July 21. The renowned Hemingway Days Festival features exciting events such as an internationally recognized short story competition, storytelling contest, and Marlin Fishing Tournament. Sloppy Joe's plays a major part during the festival by sponsoring the Hemingway Look-Alike Contest.

During this contest gentlemen that resemble the bearded larger than life Ernest Hemingway compete to be named "Papa" for that year's celebration. The 2016 recipient of this honor is David Hemingway, no relation, of North Carolina. This year was his 7th attempt for the coveted award and indeed seven was a lucky number for him. The Papas as they are known are celebrities in their own right and are the popular man about town for this week long celebration. According to this year's Papa, David Hemingway, they are followed around Key West by camera crews, groupies, and autograph seekers. Everyone wants their picture taken with a Papa.

The Hemingway Look Alikes do have a loftier goal than to just party like Papa. They raise money for college scholarships through fundraising during the event with the Silent Auction being one of the biggest fundraising events. According to Hemingway, donated items such as chef Paul Menta's locally made rum, handmade models of the Ernest Hemingway fishing yacht The Pilar, and other items bring in a lot of money, all for a great cause. The good times start when the doors swing open at 9:00 am daily and noon on Sundays. Serving a diverse menu of Caribbean-American food, it also includes bar favorites such as burgers, sandwiches, and salads. Be sure to wash down your delicious meals with one of SJ's generous signature drinks such as the Sloppy Rita, Frozen Bacardi Light Rum Runner, Sloppy Mojito, or Papa Dobles (Papa's favorite!).

Kenny Chesney loves Key West and Sloppy Joe's on Duval Street. He held his Keg in the Keys concert here on March 21, 2016 to a more than capacity crowd and used the opportunity to get tuned up for his upcoming U.S. Tour. He usually brings along a few friends and this year was no exception. Country star Eric Church, Old Dominion's Matthew Ramsey, and NASCAR's Dale Earnhardt, Jr. joined Kenny for this special night of music and fun. Photo Credit: Jill Trunnell

FOGARTY'S

227 Duval Street
(305) 294-7525
Daily 11:00 a.m. – 1:00 a.m.
www.fogartysofkeywest.com

Located on the corner of Caroline and Duval Street, you'll find a place that has some of the finest food in town and is more fun than a barrel of monkeys. Fogarty's is one of the most popular spots on Duval Street where you can dine al fresco while people watching and keeping cool with a frozen drink from the Flying Monkey Bar. You can also choose to dine inside the 1880s era mansion, which is reported to be haunted, in the air-conditioning and choose from a large menu of island favorites.

Fogarty's has been serving up fabulous food and fun since 2003 in the former home of Dr. Joseph Fogarty, a prominent member of Key West society and mayor in the early 1900s. Located a short walk from the cruise ship docks its always popular with the day trippers, but it's perfect for any occasion, Spring Break, Fantasy Fest, or just any day of the week.

Their appetizers are sure to do just that, tempt your appetite, because the menu reads like a who's who of great bar food choices. Choose from golden fried Mahi-Mahi bites, peel and eat shrimp, Key West Crab Cakes, Tex Mex Rolls, Buffalo Chicken Tenders, and others. They offer more than six different salads such as Chinese Chicken, Caesar, Ahi, Santa Fe, and Fogarty's Chopped Salad.

You better bring a hardy appetite because Fogarty's has a great reputation for bringing generous portions to the table. They have wonderful sandwiches such as Dolphin Grilled, Fogarty Fish Sandwich, Shrimp and Bacon Club, Duval Club, and a couple of Burger choices. The Dolphin sandwich is grilled and seasoned with lemon and herbs, grilled onions, lettuce, and tomato. The Shrimp and Bacon Club makes my mouth water just thinking about its grilled Gulf Shrimp with smoked bacon, Swiss cheese, lettuce, tomato, and tomato basil dressing. The Duval Club is piled high with turkey, ham, and

Swiss cheese, with crisp bacon, lettuce, tomato, and mayonnaise on toasted wheat bread.

They offer a couple of different soups, the soup of the day and the Bahamian Conch and Clam Chowder. The Bahamian Chowder is prepared with a tasty mix of tomatoes, potatoes, carrots, celery, island spices of lots of conch, and clams from the sea.

The entrée section reads like a cross section of the peoples that make up population of Key West itself with a nice mix of seafood, Caribbean dishes, and of course some traditional American favorites. Choose from local seafood choices such as pecan encrusted Mahi-Mahi, Fogarty's mixed grill, Baha Fish Tacos, and Fish of the Day. You can't go wrong with any of these dishes. From our island neighbor to the south they offer Cuban Style Roast Pork served with traditional rice and beans with fried plantains. They also offer a fine aged beef filet mignon with side of mashed potatoes and a vegetable garnish. Finally, they also have a platter of succulent slow roasted baby back ribs with sweet and smoky BBQ sauce also served with mashed potatoes, onion rings, and cole slaw.

Remember I said Fogarty's was more fun than a barrel of monkeys? I was referring to their "World Famous" Flying Monkeys bar and the bevy of frozen beverages that they serve. They make great frozen drinks with twenty different flavors offered up in three different sizes. The smallest is served in a 16 ounce souvenir cup, with the next size being a 22 ounce squeeze bottle. If you're really thirsty you may want to graduate to the jumbo 32 ounce tumbler with handle. You may need a handle after consuming the jumbo because not only are their drinks flavorful, but they also pack a punch. Just listen to the names of some of their frozen concoctions: Rum Runner, Third Degree Burn, Howler, Grape Ape, Banana Breeze, Chocohol, Dirty Monkey, and of course the Flying Monkey. In addition to all of these frozen drinks they do offer a full working bar which serves up a wide selection of beer and wine. They also offer mixed drinks made with top shelf liquors and all of the classic island cocktails that you would expect to be available in this island paradise.

Front porch and patio of Fogarty's located at 227 Duval Street. Photo courtesy of Fogarty's.

HALF SHELL RAW BAR

231 Margaret Street
Key West, Florida 33040.
305-294-7496.
Monday thru Thursday 11:00 a.m. – 10:00 p.m.
Friday thru Saturday 11:00 a.m. – 11:00 p.m.
Sunday 12:00 p.m. – 10:00 p.m.
Happy Hour is Daily 4:30p.m. – 6:30 p.m.
www.halfshellrawbar.com

With a long and storied history as a destination on Key West's waterfront, and most recently featured on the cover of Kenny Chesney's hit single, *When I See This Bar*, the Half Shell Raw Bar embodies everything good about the laid-back lifestyle of the Florida Keys. No pretense here, just easy going people with a passion for life and living it to the fullest with their friends.

The Half Shell has been in business on the Historic Key West waterfront since the early 70s and naturally became a favorite of Captains and locals due to its central location and being surrounded by the Key West commercial fishing fleet. The same holds true today as well as being a favorite dining destination for tourists and locals alike.

As you you're heading toward the Half Shell Raw Bar you can see the seafood being unloaded from the day's catch into the Half Shell Fish Market. You see they own their own seafood market which supplies all of their needs plus their sister restaurants therefore insuring the freshest and finest quality products are always available. In fact, they are the only restaurant in town that owns its seafood market.

Walk into the bar and you'll see the extensive draft beer taps, a large sailfish sculpture, and license plates from all over the world covering the walls. The well-worn barstools provide an inviting place to sit and chill with a favorite beverage and recount the day's events with friends and plan new adventures. The Half Shell is a mecca beckoning to all of those looking to experience that Caribbean cool easy-going lifestyle just like Chesney sings about in his songs.

The Half Shell Raw Bar is the original Key West fish house and offers such mouthwatering delights as broiled garlic oysters, fish and chips, steamed middle neck clams, chilled Key West peel and eat shrimp, and one of its specialties, authentic conch ceviche. Just imagine dining on the freshest seafood around while looking out over emerald green waters and the golden Key West sunset. Why not enjoy one of their signature drinks as the sun goes down. Try the Bayou Bloody Mary made with a jalapeno infused vodka, homemade bloody mary mix, and old bay seasoning on the rim, served with a celery stalk and a peel and eat shrimp. The Oyster Shooter contains a shucked oyster, jalapeno infused vodka, horseradish and cocktail sauce all in a souvenir shot glass. Looking for something a little exotic? Then try the Voodoo Juice, a special blend of four flavored rums with a tropical fruit juice blend. Who knows....you might even strike up a conversation with one of Key West leading charter captains and book yourself a fishing trip for the next day. Many of the local fishermen frequent the bar at Happy Hour which is daily from 4:30 p.m. till 6:30 p.m. and features 2-for-1 specials.

If you're looking for a true Key West original and not the same old cookie cutter establishment, amble on over to the Half Shell Raw Bar. They have all the ingredients for a special Old Key West experience...the only thing missing is you.

Half Shell Raw Bar is on the waterfront at the Historic Key West Seaport. Great dining just a few feet from where the fresh seafood comes in. Photo credit Mark Lee.

Waterfront Brewery

201 William Street
(305)440-2270
Open Daily 11 a.m. till late
www.thewaterfrontbrewery.com

The Waterfront Brewery is one of the newer bar/restaurants in this guide. It was opened in 2015 by Joe Walsh and Winnie DeMent who already own and operate four other great Key West destinations. I originally picked up on the fact that this establishment was on the way in the Fall of 2014 when we were down gathering pictures for my first book. I saw this huge box of a building with its eye-catching Weiland mural on the side and asked what was happening here. I found out that this was the former Waterfront Market and it would soon be transformed into a cool waterfront brew pub restaurant. I thought what a great location right here on the Historic Key West waterfront where I like to spend a lot of my time when I'm in town.

I recently had the chance to dine here and was really impressed with their food, drink, and service. I was in town entertaining a large party that was down here from my hometown and was their de facto tour guide for the week. With their boat being docked in the marina just down the walkway from the Waterfront Brewery it seemed a natural choice. As we walked in from the docks, I was pleased to see that this was an open-air restaurant and the back wall that overlooked the marina provided a great view of all the boats that were tied up just outside. My party was seated right away as we were greeted by the staff which was both friendly and accommodating of our large party.

At our table, we ordered the Buffalo chicken wings and the Front Street shrimp which were both wonderful. The wings were large and spicy and came with blue cheese dressing for dipping. The shrimp were fried and tossed in a Thai remoulade and judging from how quickly the plate became empty were one of our favorites. As you would expect they have some tasty shrimp and seafood dishes and the peel and eat shrimp did not disappoint. Others in my party enjoyed such dishes as Joe's Ribs, Chicken Portabella Pasta, and the Chop House Burger which all smelled and looked great. I toned it down with my dinner choice after all those great appetizers and chose the Cobb Salad which was not only delicious, but a more than generous portion size.

Looking down the menu they have a couple of tasty soups, the Bahamian White Conch Chowder and a Cuban Black Bean Soup. They also prepare a variety of salads including a Kale and Caesar. They have about ten different sandwiches on the menu for the heartier appetite. Just to name some of them, they have a catch of the day, shrimp and avocado, Waterfront Cuban sandwich, and BBQ Pork served on a Kaiser bun. The Waterfront Brewery has a couple different steak options and a number of fresh seafood dishes. They prepare a nut crusted Mahi, catch of the day, and whole fried hogfish. Shrimp is also in-offered three different ways, Shrimp and Scallop Risotto, Bayou Shrimp, and Fried Shrimp and Scallops.

As the name says, it's also a working brewery and they have around a dozen craft brewed beers that they make on tap at any given time as well as several other popular choices made by other brewers. The Waterfront Brewery does not just serve beer, they also offer wine and mixed drinks. Be sure to get there early for their bar specials. They have Happy Hour daily from 4 till 6:30. During this time all the Waterfront Brewery beers, well drinks, and wines by the glass are half price.

If you have room left after these gastronomic delights, they offer a variety of desserts sure to tempt. Choose from such favorites as authentic Key Lime Pie, decadent chocolate cake, or the cheesecake of the day.

This great new destination on Williams Street certainly lives up to its motto. They proudly state, "At the Waterfront Brewery no one goes hungry or thirsty." I know I certainly didn't. What a great night of food and fun we had here. It's now on my list of go to places on the Historic Key West waterfront.

This Wyland Mural graces the side of the Waterfront Brewery at the Historic Key West Seaport. Photo credit Mark Lee.

SALUTE ON THE BEACH

1000 Atlantic Blvd
(305) 292-1117
Lunch 11:30a.m.-4:30 p.m.
Dinner 5:00p.m. -9:30 p.m.
Bar open 11:00 a.m. -10:30 p.m.
www.saluteonthebeach.com

Salute is a waterfront restaurant located on Higg's Beach and provides a relaxing view of the ocean plus some delicious Italian and seafood dishes. Salute is the sister restaurant to the much beloved, Blue Heaven, and provides a light Caribbean influenced take on some Italian classics. Found between the White Street pier and the Casa Marina Hotel, Salute combines two of my favorite things, Italian food and the beach.

We took an afternoon break here after a long scooter ride out to Fort East Martello and had an appetizer of Stone Crab Claws with cocktails and soaked up some of the beach vibe as we relaxed in the open-air dining area. Salute is known for its fresh breads, vegetables, and local seafood. It is open for both lunch and dinner and serves outstanding food with the backdrop of the Atlantic Ocean.

Some of their choices for appetizers on the lunch menu are steamed mussels in bianco, calamari in marinara, peel and eat shrimp, and Carrie's gazpacho. They also have a variety of salads including Caprese, Shrimp, or Spinach. Their sandwiches are crazy good and you can choose from Yellowtail Snapper, chicken breast, hamburger, or antipasti which is a variety of Italian meats and cheese with peppers and onions.

For the more traditional Italian choices, you can have pasta and vegetables in pesto sauce or spaghetti and meatballs in marinara sauce.

The dinner menu is stocked with a hardier selection on entrees.

You'll find such classics as pasta carbonara that can be dressed up with chicken, shrimp, or scallops. There is also Spaghetti with meatballs as well as homemade lasagna with meat sauce. For the seafood lover, there are plenty of choices such as linguini with mussels in a white wine and butter sauce. Try the Chef Denis' Ditalini and Cheese with sautéed Key West Shrimp. There is also sautéed scallops on fresh greens with tropical salsa and a sautéed yellowtail snapper with lemon cream sauce and spinach. For a lighter fare, there is a nightly vegetable plate with potatoes, Brussel sprouts, beans, and tofu.

For dessert, they have Key Lime Pie, Dan's Cheesecake, chocolate mousse, and a homemade chocolate chip cookie ice cream sandwich.

The bar is open all day and closes at 10:30 in the evening providing a full-service selection of cocktails, beer, and wine. Salute is another one of those places that I had passed a hundred times traveling around Key West and just never had stopped to try it out. With the combination of being beachfront with abundant sunshine and having some great Italian food, Salute has a lot of pluses and is a terrific addition to the list of places I would recommend trying in Key West!

Salute is a cool Italian restaurant on scenic Higg's Beach. Photo credit Mark Lee.

MARGARITAVILLE

500 Duval Street
(305) 292-1435
Open Daily; 11 am – 12am
www.margaritavillekeywest.com

Margaritaville is a place where it's always summer, the beer is ice cold, and you can drop in anytime of the year and enjoy a laid back afternoon at the "beach." Grab a cheeseburger off the grill with fries and try a margarita from their signature blenders. Margaritaville's menu runs the gamut from appetizers, soups and salads, sandwiches, entrees, to of course, a variety of cheeseburgers. Dive into their drink menu which includes ten different kinds of margaritas, shooters, boat drinks, a multitude of beers including Land Shark, and a full wine list. The drink list draws inspiration from some of Jimmy Buffett's songs including names such as the Last Mango in Paris margarita, Five O' Clock Somewhere Boat Drink, and Don't Stop the Carnival frozen drink.

In business in Key West since 1985, The Margaritaville Store first opened at 4 Lands End Village and offered the t-shirts, beads, and trinkets that all of those Buffett fans came in search of. When the store first opened there was no restaurant or bar, and if you've ever listened to Jimmy Buffet you know that he is famous for a couple of songs that refer to food and drink, namely cheeseburgers and margaritas.

Realizing that these integral appetites were going unsatisfied and also that they were quickly outgrowing their building; The Margaritaville Store moved to its present site at 500 Duval Street in the former S.H. Kress building where it was joined by the Margaritaville Cafe.

At the December 1987 opening of the Margaritaville Cafe on Duval Street, Jimmy Buffett quipped, "When I started out playing bars in this town, all I wanted was enough money to buy a boat I could sail away on if success faded. The other alternative was to buy my own bar so I could hire myself and just keep singing. Welcome to Margaritaville!" And as they say the rest is history. Key West is the site of the first successful Margaritaville and my how the empire has grown since its humble beginnings as a T Shirt shop. The Margaritaville Label now graces hotels, resorts, and casinos as well as more restaurants across the country and the Caribbean.

Contrary to popular belief, Jimmy Buffet still goes down to Key West and The Florida Keys. I saw him myself perform a concert for a few thousand Parrot Heads at a beachfront venue. He also has a recording studio called Shrimpboat Sound hiding in plain site where he comes to lay down tracks for his albums. You may or may not run into Jimmy on your visit to Key West, but you will definitely find a good time at Margaritaville.

Rumor has it that this fellow and his band may get to christen the new Key West Amphitheatre some-time in 2018. Photo credit Mark Lee.

JACK FLATS

509.5 Duval Street
305-294-7955
Open Daily 11am till late
www.jackflatskw.com

It has become a November tradition for my wife and me to go down to Key West for the Meeting of the Minds. For the uninitiated that is the yearly gathering of the Phlock of Jimmy Buffett faithful known as the Parrot Heads. This takes place the first full week of November with the Casa Marina serving as the headquarters of some partying with a purpose and a whole lot of good music. Sometimes there's even an appearance by Buffet himself. Anyway, since it's college football season we go on Saturday afternoons for lunch to this cool place that we found a few years ago known as Jack Flats. We like to kick back with a few drinks and appetizers and cheer on our favorite team, the Georgia Bulldogs. Jack Flats is located in the heart of Duval Street in Old Town Key West at 509 ½ Duval Street almost directly across from Margaritaville.

For the sports enthusiast, I can think of no better place to be. Jack Flats has 19 big screen TVs on which to enjoy watching your favorite game and your selection from their delicious menu and a cold beverage. To say that their portions are generous would be an understatement. My plate was piled high with a mound of tots the height of Everest and the sandwiches are large enough to share or satisfy the hardiest appetite. They have an extensive appetizer menu with crowd pleasing favorites such as Buffalo Wings, Jacks Nachos, and US 1 Sliders. The local seafood supply lends itself to such selections as Buffalo or Coconut Shrimp, Jacks Fish Bites, and Blackened Mahi Sliders. Jacks has six different salads to choose from and you can choose from a variety of sandwiches. They have great burgers, and seafood sandwiches made with dolphin, shrimp, or grouper. Each sandwich comes with either French fries or sweet potato fries or you can have a mound of tater tots for just a dollar extra. Try one of their eight Blue Plate specials which range from Jack's Meatloaf to Jack's Sirloin steak, grilled to order with mash potatoes and broccoli. You'll also find more Blue Plate favorites such as Chicken Parm, Fish and Chips, Jack's Shepherd Pie, and Margarita Chicken. Last but certainly not least, make sure to save room for a piece of either their scrumptious Key Lime Pie or Chocolate Cake. If you are a sports enthusiast or just looking for some great food which is big on flavor and portion, you can't go wrong with Jack Flats.

The San Carlos Institute is a Cuban cultural center located on Duval Street across from Jack Flats. Photo credit Mark Lee.

CAPTAIN TONY'S SALOON

428 Greene Street
(305) 294-1838
Open Daily 10 am – 2 am
www.capttonyssaloon.com

Housed in a building dating back to 1851, this bar has a history almost as colorful as its namesake, Captain Tony Tarracino. This site served as an ice house in the days before electricity came to the Keys and as the city morgue. Home to Key West's 'Hanging Tree", it was the sight of over 15 deaths including pirates and one woman. This woman came to be known as the infamous 'lady in blue' and it is said that her spirit still haunts Captain Tony's to this day.

In the 1890s it housed a telegraph station where the news of the battleship Maine's explosion in Cuba was received. Later in the early 1900s it served as a cigar factory and during prohibition was a speakeasy called the Blind Pig which served up gambling, women, and bootleg rum called Hoover Gold.

Most notably, this is the original site of Sloppy Joe's which is famous for being Ernest Hemingway's favorite daily watering hole in Key West. Opened by Joe "Josie" Russell in 1933 after the end of prohibition it served as a spot of rest, storytelling, and occasional drama on the local Key West stage. It was only after a dispute over a rent increase of $1 and a clause in the lease stating that all fixtures must stay if he ended the lease, that he decided to move the bar in the middle of the night, customers and fixtures included, to its present day location at the corner of Duval and Greene Streets. An interesting side note is that Hemingway insisted on claiming the bar's urinal in the move and relocated it to his home at 907 Whitehead Street, where it can still be seen today and is used as a watering trough for his beloved six-toed cats.

In 1958, the bar was purchased by Tony Tarrancino, a New Jersey transplant who had originally came to Key West for his "health." The story is told that Tony had been very successful with the horses out at the Garden State Race Track. He and his brothers figured out that they could get the results of the races with their dad's new TV before the bookies could and they were winning a bundle. When the mob got wind of this they took Tony on a little "one way ride" out to the landfill and left him for dead after a good beating. When Tony woke up the next day he figured it would be better for his longevity if he left town. He headed south and came all the way down to Key West where he started a new life.

Captain Tony worked as a shrimper, charter boat captain, and was the even mayor of Key West, but is known far and wide for his Saloon at 428 Greene Street. Captain Tony passed away in 2008, but his spirit lives on. His bar has changed little and still has ladies' bras on its ceiling and business cards fill the posts around the bar and every bar stool is painted with the name of a famous person who not only sat on it, but also was a regular at the bar. There's live entertainment every afternoon and a live band every night and always a great crowd of locals and tourists alike.

Captain Tony's has become an institution in Key West and a must visit destination on your itinerary.

Night time at Captain Tony's on Greene Street. Photo credit Mark Lee.

THE SCHOONER WHARF BAR

202 William Street
(305)292-3302
Open 7am – 4 am, SEVEN DAYS A WEEK
www.schoonerwharf.com

Often referred to as "a last little piece of Old Key West," and voted the Best Locals Bar six years in a row, you can't go wrong when you choose The Schooner Wharf. According to the bar's website, it was originally located on the Schooner Diamante and its top shelf liquor was kept in the top drawer of the file cabinet behind the bar. The Schooner has since been relocated and expanded on shore into a neighboring building and added a second story deck which overlooks the historic Key West waterfront and its yachts and sailboats.

A favorite of the Beach Boy's Al Jardine, it was also the choice watering hole of treasure salvor Mel Fisher, a legend in his own right. The Schooner's rustic charm and locals flavor appealed to this local hero who sought out and found the treasure of the Atocha, full of gems, coins, and precious metals, nearby in the waters off the Florida Keys. Charles Kuralt, the late CBS journalist, stated when referring the Schooner that "this must be the center of the universe."

With is waterfront location and nautical motif, you'll enjoy some of the freshest seafood around. Fresh Stone crab claws, peel-and-eat shrimp, fresh-shucked oysters, and, of course, Conch chowder and fritters, are among the local seafood delicacies on the menu in the galley. For the land lovers of your crew you'll find a bountiful assortment of appetizers, burgers, chicken, soups, and salads.

The Schooner Wharf offers two different happy hours throughout the day: From 7 a.m.-noon and 5-7 p.m. Check out the extensive frozen and tropical drink menu, as well as a bountiful bevy of beers http://schoonerwharf.com/pdf/2016drinkmenu.pdf.

The Schooner Wharf is an active part of the community and sponsors numerous events throughout the year such the Lighted Boat Parade in December, the Minimal Regatta over the Memorial Day weekend, Wrecker's Cup Race Series, Barbecue Cook-off, Chili Cook-off, and one of the Keys' favorite local events, the Battle of the Bars. Entertainment abounds and will be sure to keep you captivated into the evening.

Frank Everhart is the in house magician and has been wowing patrons for the past 20 years with his up close magic and slight of hand. He performs five days a week so be sure to come any evening Wednesday thru Sunday with magic commencing at 9 p.m. If its music that gets you started, you'll find a variety of melodic entertainment starting every day at noon and running late into the night. Be sure to check the website, http://www.schoonerwharf.com/entertainment.htm, for the latest schedule of entertainers coming to the Schooner Wharf stage.

Scenic Key West waterfront found just to the right of the Schooner Wharf Bar. Photo credit Mark Lee.

THE CORK AND STOGIE

1218 Duval Street
(305) 517-6419
Open somewhere around 10 a.m.
Noonish Sunday till we close usually in the 11 p.m. range
www.corkandstogie.com

In an unassuming two story, white house on lower Duval Street, you'll find the Cork and Stogie a place to come hang out and catch up with old friends and meet new ones. Its wide inviting porch calls to you on the sidewalk and you can't help yourself as you climb the steps up to the bar and order a cool drink and have a seat. Its friendly helpful staff will make you feel welcome and so will the eclectic blend of local customers who frequent this chilled hangout on the less rowdy end of Duval.

The Cork and Stogie has been open since 2009 and is a cool local's bar which welcomes tourists alike. It's a craft beer mecca and offers, depending on the time, 60 to 70 different beers and as many as 130. They also have an extensive wine list with over 50 to choose from sourced from such countries as New Zealand, Russia, South Africa, Argentina, and more.

I was first introduced to the Cork and Stogie when I learned that friend and local musician, Chris Rehm was investing in this bar a couple of years ago. Chris comes to Key West via Miami where he lived for more than 20 years. After a successful career in the luxury auto business he decided to make the move down US 1 to Key West where he has lived for about nine years. Chris loves island life and he is just one of the things about the Cork and Stogie that makes it a cool place to hang out. Often you can find him on the porch chilling with his better half and musical partner, Dani Hoy, between one of their music gigs that they play locally with their band, The Shanty Hounds.

The Cork and Stogie, as its name references, also has a primo selection of fine cigars such as Arturo Fuente, CAO, Joya de Nicaragua, and Padron. To further enhance your smoking pleasure, they also offer accessories for sale such as cutters, ashtrays, and humidors.

The front porch has comfortable seating and tables for relaxing and taking in all the sights and sounds of Duval Street. Whether it's chickens clucking back and forth or the occasional procession of scooter riding tourists there's always something to see. Sit back and relax with your favorite beer or wine and talk with friends. The Cork and Stogie also has books by local authors and is even frequented by some of them. Come by one afternoon and plan to stay a while. You may just find your new regular locals place. Even if you're not a local just pretend and live like one for a day.

The Cork and Stogie on Duval is a great stop for a cold beer and a cigar! Photo credit Mark Lee.

HOG'S BREATH SALOON

400 Front Street
(305) 296-4222
Open Daily 10 am – 2 am
www.hogsbreath.com/keywest

The world famous Hog's Breath Saloon has been serving its thirsty patrons for almost 30 years in the heart of Key West and a stone's throw from the waterfront and Mallory Square.

Not to drop names, but recently in March 2013, Kenny Chesney chose to kick off his latest US tour here at the Hog's Breath. He held an impromptu concert billed at Kegs in the Keys and played for a crowd of about 5000, who were shoulder to shoulder on the patio, bar, and spilling into the street as he wowed the crowd in one of his favorite locations to be, Key West.

Originally started in 1976 by Jerry Dorminy in Ft. Walton Beach, FL as somewhere to hang out with his friends after a hard day of sailing and fishing, he branched out in 1988 and thus was born the Hog's Breath in Key West. He was looking for somewhere known for its watersports and fishing like Fort Walton and Key West was the perfect fit. It has great fishing, diving, and the night life has an energy all its own. Since its inception, the Hog's Breath has been popular with the locals and the place where tourists go to try and fit in and taste a little bit of the local flavor.

It offers a full menu of favorites including appetizers such as Buffalo Hogs Wings, Bahamian Conch Chowder, and Seafood Sampler. Its entrees are crowd pleasing favorites such as a full range of sandwiches and dinner portions of mahimahi, shrimp, or crab. Don't forget the Raw bar where you'll find oysters by the dozen, shrimp, and stone crab (when in season.) Also try one of the signature drinks such as the Hog Snort, the Hogarita, or Havana Hog Punch. Prices are reasonable and portions are generous. Comes as you are and blend in with the locals at the Hog's Breath.

THE GREEN PARROT

601 Whitehead Street
(305) 294-6133
Open 10 a.m. – 4 a.m., Seven Days a Week
Happy Hour Daily
Monday thru Thursday 4 p.m. – 7 p.m.
Friday 4 p.m. – 5:30 p.m.
www.greenparrot.com

Green Parrot, the name conjures up images in your mind of something colorful, tropical, and certainly out of the ordinary. It usually inhabits exotic tropical islands loaded with beautiful wildlife and is often surrounded by emerald green waters. Sounds like you could also be describing the Green Parrot Bar located just off the main drag at the corner of Southard and Whitehead Streets in Key West.

The Green Parrot has been referred to by Playboy magazine as "the definitive Key West saloon" and was named in their Top Twenty Bars of America. It has also garnered a certificate of excellence from the respected Trip Advisor website. With a timeless atmosphere and an open air feel, it may seem that very little has changed since the building was occupied by its first resident. Originally constructed in 1890, the building served as the grocery store of local merchant Antonio Sanchez, as well as the boyhood home of renowned folk artist Mario Sanchez, Antonio's grandson. The transition to saloon occurred in the 1940s when the Brown Derby opened to serve the thirsty navy submarine crews who were stationed in Key West. Sailors who were stationed here who returned in later years have remarked that they can barely find the former navy base but felt right at home once they got back to the "old Brown Derby."

The Navy left in the early seventies and so did the name with the venerable saloon returning as The Green Parrot. Key West was quickly becoming a mecca for the artists, bikers, free spirits, and otherwise nonconformists. The Parrot became a place where old sailors and old hippies were welcome and could be found side by side at the bar.

Music has always figured prominently in the appeal of the Green Parrot. Starting in the days of Antonio Sanchez, local Latin musicians would have informal jam sessions, called descargas, in the back room of his grocery store. Today the Green Parrot offers some of the hottest performers around and has been recognized by Zagat Survey as the Number One Music Venue in South Florida. Any given weekend you can find a nationally recognized touring band performing on the stage and during the week the jukebox cranks out the tunes as you enjoy a game of darts, pool, or pinball and some complimentary popcorn. If you've worked up a thirst, try one of their signature drinks the Green Parrot Root Beer Barrel, made with Root Beer Schnapps and beer. The Green Parrot is known for its great drinks and ice cold beer and you never know who you might meet sitting on the barstool next to you. For a unique experience and a chance to rub elbows with tourists and locals alike, come on over and have a drink at the Green Parrot tonight.

Grab a drink and a game of pool at the Green Parrot at the corner of Truman and Whitehead. Photo credit Mark Lee.

THE PORCH

429 Caroline Street
(305) 517-6358
11 a.m. – 4 a.m., 7 days a week, 363 days a year
www.theporchkw.com

The Porch is truly a hidden gem of Key West, found just outside the fray of Duval at 429 Caroline Street. Opened in July 2010 by well-known Key West author, Chris Shultz, and Keith St. Peter, it is housed in the historic Porter Mansion. This Victorian structure is so named for Dr. Joseph Porter its former owner and resident who is said to have been born and died in the same upstairs room. As the story goes, Dr. Porter, the first native born Key West physician was also the state of Florida's first medical officer. One of the most common diseases of his time was malaria and when his patients died he would often put dimes on their eyes. His ghost still reportedly inhabits The Porch today and is said to upon occasion throw glasses about the room and leave dimes on the bar. Originally constructed in 1838, the Porter mansion has been on the U.S. National Register of Historic Places since 1973.

The Porch is a mecca for the craft beer aficionado and offers over 18 draft and 50 plus bottles of the finest beers from the U.S. and international sources. The draft beer list is refreshed on a regular basis to offer the beer lover a chance to savor new experiences and keep up with the latest brews. They also have an extensive wine list with 12 wines by the glass and a well-appointed selection of over 70 bottles to drink or carry home for later. Of course their friendly and knowledgeable staff is always there to steer you in the right direction. Noted to be a locals kind of place and very popular with the off duty bartenders of the island, you'll always have plenty of advice as to the best and latest beers to try. If you feel like taking a walk outside it's ok to grab a chair and enjoy your brew or fruit of the vine al fresco on the large and inviting wrap around porch.

I will only quote a few of the reviews found on the Facebook site of The Porch lest I cause a stampede of bargoers and totally screw up the ambience and casual appeal of this place. Past patrons have said this, "great vibes, good people and best of all good beer, "and "perfect spot to get away from the madness,", and of course my personal favorite, "delicious beer will magically appear." The Porch has been featured in such publications as the New York Times, Southern Living, and Gun and Garden.

The Porch is housed in the historic Porter Mansion, just go to the left at the top of the stairs. Photo credit Mark Lee.

THE CHART ROOM

1 Duval Street

(305) 296-4600

Daily 4:30 p.m. – 2:00 a.m.

Happy Hour 4:30 p.m. – 6:00 p.m.

www.pierhouse.com/Dining/chart_room.asp

On its website the Pier House Resort refers to the Chart Room as "a weird little bar trapped inside a luxury resort." It has been said by many that the Chart Room is such an integral and beloved part of Key West that the Pier House literally developed around it.

Since 1968, with a quirky character all its own, the Chart Room Bar has stood the test of time at Key West's waterfront. Once the regular watering hole of such literary luminaries as Tennessee Williams, Truman Capote, and Hunter S. Thompson it holds a special place in the hearts of locals and guests of the Pier House Resort. Local legend has it that Jimmy Buffett crafted his laid back tropical style of music by playing for drinks in the Chart Room in his early Key West days. He polished his style while singing for treasure divers, beach goers, politicians, and friends. In fact both Jimmy Buffett and Bob Marley played their first gigs here.

Carol Shaugnessy of the Florida Keys News Bureau interviewed Chris Robinson, former Chart Room bartender and this was his take on Key West and the role that the Chart Room played. "Politicos ran the government largely from the Chart Room Bar, pot smugglers were admired as romantic outlaws, and local treasure hunters drank rum with Pulitzer-winning escapees from the literary mainstream." Long since retired from his bartending days and spending off time adventures with the likes of Jimmy Buffett and Hunter Thompson, Robinson now spends his days on the local waters working as a fishing guide on his own boat.

Key West has changed a lot since its renegade days of the 70s and you probably would have better luck finding the local politicians at City Hall. However, the Chart Room still holds court on the waterfront for tourists and locals alike. It's open daily from 4:30 p.m. till 2:00 a.m. with Happy Hour from 4:30 p.m. till 6:00 p.m. Come by, grab a bar stool, and have a drink and enjoy its signature free popcorn, peanuts, and hot dogs. Just don't ask for one of those blender drinks with the cute little umbrellas. They don' have a blender or umbrellas...just cool drinks, great company, and a good time.

Behind this mild mannered façade lives one of the coolest bars in town! Photo credit Mark Lee.

One of a kind 1970's time warp known as The Chart Room. One of the coolest bars you find in town. Photo courtesy of The Pier House Resort.

HOG FISH BAR AND GRILL

6810 Front Street
Stock Island, FL 33040
(305) 293-4041
Monday thru Saturday 11 a.m. – 11 p.m.
Sunday 8 a.m. – 11 p.m.
www.hogfishbar.com

Take a short little drive, just off Key West over Cow Channel Bridge, down Front Street, past a row of rusty old trailers, and you stumble upon a part of the Keys that time has forgotten. Here in Safe Harbor Marina you'll find the Hog Fish Bar and Grill, where locals bring their out of town friends to show them what Key West used to be like before development came.

Situated on the waterfront next to the marina that is rumored to have served as the headquarters for the Bay of Pigs Invasion of Cuba in the 1960s, the Hogfish serves up fresh local seafood and strong drink. The establishment takes its name from the delicious, but often hard to come by fish of the same moniker. The motto around Key West on hogfish, a flaky, delicate, white-fleshed fish, is "we have it when we have it." It's native to these waters, but it's hard to come by: not only does it have to be speared by a diver, but it's also seasonal.

If you like seafood, you'll find no fresher. Dine on peel and eat shrimp and drink ice cold beer as you watch the shrimp boats pull back into the marina freshly loaded with the catch of the day. Sitting at your waterfront table or tiki style booth, you'll have the perfect perch to witness all the comings and goings along the waterfront and the perfect vantage point to welcome the arrival of evening as the sun slowly sinks out of view.

The Hogfish Bar and Grill has been featured on the Today show with Matt Laurer and Al Roker. It was also on a segment of Adam Richman's Man vs Food. A favorite of locals for its Old Key West appeal, it has attracted such notables as Jimmy Buffet, Paula Dean, and Vanilla Ice. Do you yourself a favor and drive on over to the Hog Fish Bar and Grill. You'll find easy to follow directions on their website.

Locals place for sure, The Hogfish Bar and Grill on Stock Island. This is like Key West before the tourists came. Photo credit by Mark Lee.

The Hog Fish Bar and Grill is surrounded by a working waterfront. Photo credit Mark Lee.

RED FISH BLUE FISH

407 Front Street
(305) 295-7447
Open Daily from 11:00 a.m. -10:00 p.m.
www.redfishbluefishkw.com

You won't have trouble finding this popular Key West Seafood house in its recently renovated bright yellow building on the corner of Wall Street and Tift's Alley. It's popular not only for its great fresh seafood, but also due to its primo location. It's within a few minutes' walk in several directions of some of Key West's most popular attractions including Mallory Square, The Mel Fisher Museum, and the Key West Aquarium.

When you walk into Red Fish Blue Fish you know that you are in a traditional old Florida seafood house due to their authentic décor and feel. Their walls are sided in varnished notty pine and covered with mounted gamefish and period signs. The bar, which was part of the renovation, was constructed from Dade County Pine which was salvaged from an old smuggler's warehouse from back in the day on Duval Street.

They serve only the freshest of seafood which is all sourced from local waters except for the Salmon which is not native to these parts. The oysters that are served are brought down from Apalachicola Bay in the panhandle of Florida. Apalachicola oysters are held in high esteem and considered some of the best in the country due to their plumpness and sweet flavor.

I see a lot of my favorites on their extensive appetizer menu. They have conch fritters, crab cakes, coconut shrimp, dolphin crispers and fried calamari. Two of the most popular appetizers here are the Key West Ceviche and the Mallory Mussels. The Key West Ceviche is made with chopped conch, shrimp, and calamari with garden vegetables in a citrus dressing with island spices and cilantro. The Mussels are prepared with fresh basil, fennel, butter, tomato, onion, garlic, spiced rum, and citrus. They also have an appetizer portion Sesame

Ahi Tuna and Front Street Shrimp which are jumbo Gulf shrimp lightly fried and tossed in a terrific Thai chili remoulade.

You'll find a couple of delicious soups if that's what you crave. They have a Creamy Corn and Crab Chowder and a Classic Conch Chowder. They also have no fewer than six different salads including Caesar, Rare Seared Ahi Tuna, Key West Cobb, and others.

If it's a sandwich that you're looking for you can pick from fresh fish, club, seafood, or burgers. They prepare a lightly seasoned and grilled Mahi-mahi sandwich and a golden fried catch of the day sandwich. I can recommend the club as well as the Shrimp Po Boy. If you're hungry you may want to go for the ¾ pound Chop House Burger. And of course, it would not be Key West without Cuban food and they have an authentic Cuban Mix on the menu made with delicious mojo pulled pork, sliced ham, white cheese, tomato, lettuce, and yellow mustard.

Finally, we've reached the entrees and I've worked up an appetite getting here. The menu is full of delicious choices, all brilliantly prepared by Chef Paul Orchard who's been with the restaurant for over 10 years. The most popular entrée is the Cioppino which is made with five delicious seafoods, Mahi-mahi, shrimp, scallops, mussels and calamari combined with tomato, fresh fennel, herbs, and a rich white wine and tomato broth. This flavorful goodness is served with a piece of bread so you don't have to waste any of its tasty soup. The menu is stocked full of other great seafood choices such as the Wall Street Hogfish which is locally caught and served with a blue crab stuffing. The Key West Grill is a sauté of sea scallops and gulf shrimp presented with their lime cilantro sauce. The Baja Mahi Tacos are soft flour tortillas stuffed with blackened grilled Mahi, grilled onions, chili cream, peppers, and cheese served with black rice and beans. There are two different shrimp and pasta dishes. They prepare a shrimp scampi that is served over angel hair pasta and Bayou Shrimp which is gulf shrimp served in a Cajun cream sauce over bowtie pasta.

Another of their specialties is the local whole Snapper which is deep fried and served with island rice, black beans, and vegetable of the day. For the landlubber, they also offer several other delicious choices including the Cuban Pulled Pork, Chicken Carbonara, and Sirloin Béarnaise.

Red Fish Blue Fish has a full bar serving a variety of beers, wines, mixed drinks, and some delicious island cocktails. Their Happy Hour is 3 p.m. – 6:30 p.m. with half priced draft beer and specialty drinks. Try one of their delightful homemade drinks made with real fruit and fresh juices from their extensive drink menu with selections like the Pina Colada, Key Lime Mojito, Sunset Margarita, or a Banana Daiquiri. They also have a couple of signature drinks called the Red Fish and the Blue Fish. The Blue Fish is made with raspberry vodka, citrus vodka, blue Curacao, sour, and a splash of 7-Up and the Red Fish is made with dark rum, coconut rum, mango rum, orange, cranberry, and pineapple juices. You're in the lower latitudes so why not give the Tropical Storm a try. It's a refreshing blend of light rum, mango rum, banana liquor, fresh orange juice, pineapple juice, and a splash of Grenadine.

Red Fish Blue Fish is a family friendly spot and it even serves its kids' meals in a little boat which your smaller diners are sure to like. If you're on lower Duval or anywhere near the Northwestern part of the island chances are you're within convenient walking distance to Red Fish Blue Fish. This would be a great choice for lunch if you're out touring around and it's also a smart pre-or post-Mallory Square Sunset Celebration spot due to its proximity. Shopping weary husbands often use it as a refuge from the sun in the summer and enjoy a frosty drink as their wives shop away in the Clinton Market next door. Lots of locals also choose to dine here so that tells me that it's really good and I think that you'll like it too.

Locals Tip: The entrance to Red Fish Blue Fish is actually on Tift's Alley. You'll find them on the corner of Tift's Alley and Wall Street. Since the renovation they've actually had no frontage on Front Street. Go figure, but all of the listings say Front Street. If you're in the vicinity of 407 Front Street just go to Tift's Alley and you're there.

Wreckers monument found around the corner from Red Fish Blue Fish. Photo credit by Mark Lee.

THE BULL AND WHISTLE BAR

224 Duval Street

(305) 296-4565

Monday – Saturday 10 a.m.- 4 a.m.

Sunday Noon – 4 a.m.

www.bullkeywest.com

The Bull is the oldest open air bar in Old Town Key West and can be found at the corner of Duval and Caroline streets. It harkens back to Key West's rough and tumble seafaring days and a good time can always be found here. Sit and wile away the day as you sip on one of your favorite beverages and people watch as the folks stroll by just outside your window. Enjoy the hand painted murals which can be found on the walls surrounding you, rich with a pictorial of Key West's golden days and historical residents.

Looking to kick things up a notch, then walk a few steps up to the Whistle Bar which is found on the second story just above the Bull. The Whistle offers some of the same fare as the Bull, only with a better view. Take in a bird's eye perspective of Old Key West as you peer over the railing of its second story balcony. Feel free to pull up a bar stool or stand at its wrought iron railing and spend a relaxing afternoon or evening sipping on your favorite drink.

Finally, if you're feeling adventurous or have worked up enough courage, you may want to wander up to the third and final floor of the Bull and Whistle which is known as the Garden of Eden.? And yes, it is just what you may be thinking. This is Key West's only clothing optional roof garden bar where clothing is not required and cameras are not welcome. Called "the best kept secret in Key West" by Rolling Stone magazine, The Garden of Eden offers live bands, body painting, drink specials, and one of the best views in town. Get there and stay till dusk and participate in their signature event, the Naked Sunset.

You'll be sure to have an unforgettable day whether you visit one or all of their bars so come by today and let one of their friendly bartenders serve you and enjoy your stay.

THE SMOKIN TUNA SALOON

4 Charles Street
(305) 517-6350
Bar Daily 10 a.m. – 2 a.m.
Raw Bar and Restaurant 11 a.m. – 10 p.m.
www.smokintunasaloon.com

The Smokin Tuna Saloon is known for its great live music and raw bar. Located just off Duval on Charles Street, you can enjoy some of the best bands around in a relaxed atmosphere. Half of the bar is covered and the remainder is located outside in a tree covered tropical patio.

The Smoking Tuna is a sponsor of the Key West Songwriters Festival which is held in May and features over 200 of the top songwriters in the country. Musicians and songwriters from all over the United States converge on the island of Key West for a week of great music and entertainment. This unique event gives the audience a chance to put a face to the music so to speak and immerse themselves in the music they might otherwise never hear. It also gives the songwriter a chance to tell his story as it may never otherwise be heard as more often than not, their creations are turned into hits by more famous musical entertainers.

The Smokin Tuna is of course famous for what else... its tuna. For starters why not try some of their signature Smokin Tuna Dip served with tortilla chips and I hear the Conch Fritters are great also. I can personally vouch for the Buffalo Wings and the peel and eat shrimp... they're both off the chain! They offer a tasty Mahi Mahi sandwich which can be had blackened or jerked. The Smokin Tuna also offers a full 1/2 pound hamburger for those with a big appetite grilled to order and served with fries. Of course they offer a full list of drinks sure to quench your thirst. Just head down Duval and veer onto Charles and you'll find the Smokin Tuna, and a smokin good time!

The Smokin Tuna is known for its great music and food. Photo credit Mark Lee.

Powerboat race week is and excellent time to visit in November. Photo credit Mark Lee with permission of Superboat International.

ISLAND DOGS

505 Front Street
305.509.7136
Open Monday 9 a.m. till close
www.islanddogsbar.com

A mere stone's throw from bustling Duval Street and just a short five minute walk from Mallory Square, you'll find this island favorite on Front Street known for its live music and great bar food. Island Dogs is an open-air bar with a relaxed come as you are atmosphere and has been serving up good times since 2005 to a mix of both tourists and locals. Due to its proximity to the waterfront and the cruise ship docking area, it is an ideal spot for the tourists who disembark to spend a day in Old Town Key West.

They specialize in tasty favorites such as local fish, pizza, and American bar food served in a "surf inspired" atmosphere surrounded by plasma screen TV's and plenty of room to hang out and mingle. As I scan down their menu I see munchies like tuna tataki, conch fritters, peel and eat shrimp, island dogs, shrimp and artichoke dip, and stone crab claws. They offer fresh succulent oysters on the half shell or chargrilled. If you're in the mood for a sandwich, you'll see there's plenty to choose from. They offer a catch of the day prepared blackened, grilled, or fried. They also serve a jerk chicken sandwich, shrimp blt, chicken Caesar wrap, fish tacos, or a traditional New England Lobstah roll. These sandwiches can be paired with a side such as a salad, fries, sautéed spinach, or coleslaw.

Remember I said they were noted for their pizzas? They offer a Key West Pizza which has white lobster sauce topped with pepperoni, shrimp, and pineapple. There is also a Buffalo Chicken Pizza served with blue cheese dressing for dipping, one of my favorites. If you want to free style it, you can build your own pizza from a selection of over twenty delicious ingredients. For those meat eaters in the group, Island Dogs offers a selection of several chargrilled burgers all made from choice Angus beef patties including the Buckhead Burger, Caribbean Burger, and the Black and Blue Burger.

To be sure, you'll have worked up quite a thirst after munching on all of these mouthwatering favorites so why not order up one of their delicious handcrafted drinks from the bar. Some of the drinks that they are known for are the Key West Mojito, Rum Runner, Goombay Smash, and a Cucumber and Ginger Martini. As great as those sound they're best known for their signature drink, the Key Lime Pie Martini. It's made with a blend of Absolut Vodka, Malibu Coconut Rum, Ke Ke Key Lime liqueur, and splash of lime juice served in a graham cracker crumb rimmed chilled martini glass. You'll also want to hop in during happy hour which is 4:30 p.m. till 6:30 p.m. Monday thru Friday. During Happy Hour they have half price specials on well drinks, house wine by the glass, and canned and bottle beer. You can also save on a selection of $5.95 bar food specials such as conch fritters, mozarella sticks, buffalo popcorn shrimp, and others.

Another thing about Island Dogs that keeps folk coming back for more is the super live music that they have every Wednesday thru Sunday night starting at 8 p.m. and playing till close. Treat yourself to live Blues music every Wednesday evening with the Larry Baeder Blues Concert Series. Larry has played with some of the legends of the Blues and each week he invites some of the local and visiting musicians to sit in with him and jam. Thursday thru Sunday they also have more great live music pulling in local musicians as well as touring talent.

Island Dogs also welcomes sports fans and it is the Southernmost hub for the Super Bowl Champ New England Patriots and the Florida State Seminoles Fan Club. Depending upon the season, you can always find something going on with fellow sports fans here.

So whether you're in town for a day and then back out to sea or staying in town for the season, you're sure to find a welcome spot at Island Dogs. Come hang out and try their delicious food and drink in a cool relaxed atmosphere. Once you give it a try, I think you'll probably be coming back for more. It's just that good.

The Key West waterfront is a busy place during Powerboat week in November. Photo by Mark Lee.

LOUIE'S BACKYARD

700 Waddell Avenue
(305) 294-1061
www.louiesbackyard.com

The first thing that I learned in real estate was location, location, location and that is but one of the many attributes that draws you to Louie's Backyard. This little piece of paradise is situated on a waterfront lot overlooking the azure green waters of the Atlantic Ocean where Waddell Avenue meets the south shore of Key West. Its Afterdeck Bar is an openair platform which not only features one of the best sunset views in town, but in the evening transforms into a romantic rendezvous, resplendent with the lights of Key West dancing on the shimmering water. However, if its beauty and location draws you there, its fabulous food, wine, and service keep you coming back for more time after time.

In 1971, this picturesque Victorian styled oceanfront home belonging to Louie Signorelli was transformed into Louie's Backyard. It was an intimate establishment that seated only 12 patrons and was serviced by one waiter and its daily receipts were kept in a cigar box. In its early days, on any given day you might bump into one of the locals such as Jimmy Buffett, Thomas McGuane, or even Hunter S. Thompson. Jimmy lived just over the fence in one of the upstairs neighboring apartments. In 1983 the property changed hands and was carefully renovated by the new owners who took great care to observe the historical integrity of the structure during the process. Due to their diligence and attention to detail, Louie's Backyard is now on the National Register of Historical Places.

Chef Doug Shook has been working his magic in the kitchen of Louie's for over 30 years and uses a blend of fresh local seafood, fruits, and vegetables. The vegetables are grown by Island Farms especially for Louie's and the fruits come freshly picked from Mr. Wong. The lobster and Key West Pink shrimp are so fresh that they were probably swimming around the local waters just yesterday. If your taste is for something besides seafood, Louie's has plenty of other choices such as choice steak, heirloom pork, lamb, and free-range chicken.

If you don't have a reservation, no worries, go to the Café' at Louie's Wine Bar which is upstairs. It has a magnificent wine list that can be enjoyed by the glass and provides what some consider the best panoramic view of the ocean on Key West. They also serve a variety of of small plates elegantly prepared to complement your wine choice and are open evenings Tuesday thru Saturday.

For an unforgettable feast for the eyes and stomach, plan an evening at Louie's Backyard.

Photo by Mark Lee.

THE SALTY ANGLER

1114 Duval Street
(305) 741-7071
Open Daily 11a.m. – 11 p.m.
www.thesaltyangler.com

This relative newcomer to Duval Street serves up a daily diet of some of the best barbeque in town and great musical talent. We spent a great evening here at the Salty Angler and think BZ and Amy run a really cool place.

The menu is loaded up with some of my BBQ favorites such as

"Meat Candy" also knows as Burnt Ends. This is brisket cubed and cooked down in au jus and Key Lime BBQ sauce until it is fall apart tender. They also have other smoked favorites such as the Brisket Plate, Pulled Pork Plate, and BBQ Spare Ribs Plate. The plates come with slaw, choice of a side, and either jalapeno cornbread muffin or brioche toast.

Salty Angler is also famous for their Thunder Thighs which is their specially prepared chicken thighs cooked low and slow with hickory wood for a delicious mouthwatering flavor.

They don't just serve barbeque alone. They also make ten different kinds of burgers some of which are made with combinations of bbq and cheese which always makes everything better. You can also get a sandwich made with anything from catch of the day, chicken, or veggie burger.

You could make a meal of the appetizers because they offer over a dozen super starters on their menu. They make excellent nachos, which are chips smothered in queso topped with your choice of pork, brisket, pinto beans, or Thunder Thighs chicken. You can also get a taco prepared with your choice of meat, Local's Catch Taco, or loaded fries smothered with their spicy queso dip and smoky bacon.

Let their highly skilled and friendly bartenders make you an adult milkshake or whatever your favorite drink is. The Salty Angler has live music every day with some of the best local and traveling musicians around. It will only take one visit here and you'll be "hooked!"

Irish Kevin's Bar

211 Duval Street
(305) 292-1262
Monday – Sunday 10 a.m. – 3:30 a.m.
www.irishkevins.com

Irish Kevin's Bar opened in 1998 by, strangely enough, three guys named Kevin. It was the musician in the bunch whose first name was borrowed and also given a nod to his "Irish heritage." The Kevins were pioneers in the late nineties when they opened their bar in Key West that featured live music and entertainers from open to close. Irish Kevin's chose a building that seems a natural for its purpose. It was once a Budweiser warehouse and later turned into the former location of a brewpub. When the Kevins took over they held onto the brew tanks for a while before moving them out in favor of the gift shop and a private balcony.

Irish Kevin's is known by the trademarked slogan: "I came, I drank, I don't remember," so how could you go wrong. It is famous for its friendly party atmosphere where the performers joke and cajole the crowd and fully encourage interaction and sing alongs. The musicians usually perform five days a week with the performer changing every four hours so if you don't like what you're hearing now, stick around and its sure to change sooner or later. A wide variety of music can be heard from their stage including modern, 50s, country, and of course Irish tunes. I've heard that a few famous faces have graced Irish Kevin's and possibly sung a tune or two including Toby Keith, Rhett Akins, Lee Brice, and Jamie Johnson.

Irish Kevin's not only serves great drinks including Guinness and Irish whiskies, but also offers a full menu of super bar food. The Gunny is said to be one of the favorites and is a sandwich comprised of smoked gouda cheese combined with smoked turkey topped with their signature "spicy mangrove mustard, " mayo, lettuce, and tomato on sweet Hawaiian bread. You may want to try one of their tasty appetizers with it such as the tater tot nachos. These nachos are made of tater tots topped with melted cheese, bacon, and jalapenos. Wow!

Irish Kevin's celebrates St. Patrick's in a big way. The weekend before St. Patrick's is a full blown celebration that leads up to the biggest Irish holiday of the year. On Saturday, Irish Kevin's opens at 7 a.m. to allow its patrons to "warm up" for the IK5K. The IK5K includes a costume contest, free drinks, breakfast, and a t-shirt to all participants. On St. Patrick's eve, there is a countdown to midnight that includes a balloon drop as twelve strikes and then on St. Pats, the bar opens again at 7a.m. for a free breakfast and all those eager beavers who want to get a jump on the day's festivities.

You don't have to wait till St. Patty's day to have a good time at Irish Kevin's. They're open every day from 10 a.m. till 2:30 a.m. serving up fun, food, and drink. Come on over today.

Irish Kevin's is located in the heart of Duval Street. Photo credit Mark Lee.

HARPOON HARRY'S

832 Caroline Street
Key West, FL 33040
(305) 294-8744
Open Seven Days a Week 6:30 a.m. – 9:00 p.m.
harpoonharryskeywest.com

What do you get when you combine a 1950s diner with a full-service bar and liquor store? You get Harpoon Harry's located at the corner of Caroline and Margaret streets right across the street from the Key West Bight. Harpoon Harrys serves up what some think is the best breakfast in town, but come anytime because they serve three meals a day.

The breakfast menu is full of such comfort food favorites as sausage gravy and biscuits, build your own omelets, and several egg and meat specials. They also have a lobster po boy, tenderloin and eggs, and eggs benedict. If it's not too early for you, pair your breakfast with a Bloody Mary or mimosa. One of their specialties on the menu is also Key Lime Pie French Toast.

If you stop by for lunch between 11 a.m. and 3 p.m., you can give one of their Blue Plate Specials a try. They can be found on the menu Monday thru Saturday. Choose from such favorites as ½ half rack BBQ ribs, roast turkey, pot roast bowl, or an open-faced steak sandwich. They also have a variety of salads, wraps, appetizers, and sandwiches.

For dinner, you'll find most of the favorites from lunch in addition to some great tasting entrees. They kick up dinner a notch with such choices as grilled 8-ounce tenderloin, grilled pork chops, fresh catch of the day, golden fried shrimp and breaded clam strips. Each of the dinner entrees comes the choice of two of the following: homemade mashed potatoes, French fries, vegetable, coleslaw, or small house salad.

My experiences with Harpoon Harry's have always been great. The waitresses are friendly and engaging, the food is plentiful, and the prices are easy on the budget. In fact, my tea glass is never empty thanks to my more than attentive waitress. Most recently I took refuge one afternoon around lunch time from a pop up thunder shower and enjoyed my lunch while planning out the rest of my Monday adventure. I had the Turkey

Club sandwich and a salad which was a lot of food. The only caveat I would point out is that Harpoon Harry's is an all cash restaurant. However, they also have an ATM if you're low on money just for your convenience.

A Key West alarm clock. Photo by Stacye Lee.

BO's FISH WAGON

801 Caroline Street
(305)294-9272
Open daily from 11:00 a.m. – 9:30 p.m.

If your headed down Caroline Street and you spot something that looks like a rusty old runaway pickup truck that just ran through a yard sale and got snagged by an old fishing net after tossing all the junk into the air and everything came down to rest in a big pile, then stop, you must be at BO's Fish Wagon the home of the best fried grouper sandwich in town.

Buddy Owen, B.O., has been serving up some of the best seafood in town since the 1970s. He started on Duval Street where he served up the best square grouper sandwich in town until he moved to his present location when he had to stop serving out of the back of a truck and have a "formal" restaurant. I use that word loosely because BO's is an open-air restaurant at the corner of the public parking lot on the Key West Bight. It's a pretty much a come as you are place which serves some great food at a reasonable price.

BO's is probably best known for their square grouper sandwich. If you're not familiar with the term 'square grouper," back in its formative years in the 1970s before Key West became the tourist mecca that it is today, the Florida Keys were awash in the drug smuggling business. If a fisherman came upon a floating bale of marijuana, also called a square grouper, out on the ocean he could greatly enhance his payday if he could take it back into town and sell it. It's that term that gives name to Buddy's delicious fish sandwich. It's lightly breaded and fried and served on a Cuban roll with a homemade Key Lime sauce with lettuce, tomato, and onion.

Another of their other specialties, the Fried Cracked Conch, is not to be missed. In addition to these treats, they also offer sandwiches made with shrimp, fish of the day, and soft-shell crab. They also have platters of grouper, fish of the day, or shrimp with sides of black beans and rice, salad, and hand-cut fries. For the land lubbers in the group they have a quarter pound fried hot dog, chicken sandwich, and the B.O.M.F. half pound Burger, Buddy Owen's Mother's Finest.

Since you're in Key West try the Key Limeade to quench your thirst or maybe a half and half with Iced Tea and Limeade. They also offer a selection of soft drinks, beer, and wine. BO's is open seven days a week from 11:00 a.m. till 9:30 p.m. If they get slow at night they close a little early. Of yeah, they only take cash so make sure to take some green with you, but not a lot. They're easy on the wallet.

Bo's Fish Wagon is on the edge of the Historic Key West Seaport. Photo credit Mark Lee.

EL SIBONEY RESTAURANT

900 Catherine Street
Key West, FL 33040
(305)296-4184
Open daily 11:00 a.m. – 9:30 p.m.
www.elsiboneyrestaurant.com

This family friendly establishment has been named Key West's Best Cuban Restaurant every year since 1993. That's quite an accolade and one that the de la Cruz family, the owners of El Siboney, cherish and wear proudly. Since 1984 the El Siboney restaurant has served locals and visitors providing authentic Cuban food with both generous portions and a budget friendly price.

You'll find this gem tucked away in a quaint residential neighborhood in Old Town Key West, but it's only a short walk or bike ride from Duval Street so it shouldn't be too hard to find at 900 Catherine Street. In that little red brick building they serve up some of the finest Cuban dishes that you'll taste this side of the Florida Straits. Their menu is extensive so you should be able to find something that you like. There are lots of beef, chicken, pork, and seafood dishes with something literally for all tastes.

Two of the most popular meals are the Roast Pork and the Siboney Steak. My personal favorite is Ropa Vieja with rice and beans, plantains, and Cuban bread. Almost all of the entrees come with choice of yellow or white rice with beans, sweet plantains, and Cuban bread or French fries, salad, and Cuban bread. If you can't handle a large platter, they have a good selection of sandwiches, perfect for lunch or a small evening meal. They have a Cuban Mix that is very good as well as Ham and Cheese, Boliche, and others. Some of their popular side dishes are conch chowder, chicken soup, cassava fried or boiled, croquetas, and chicken or beef empanada. For your beverage, you can choose from soft drinks, tea, or coffee as well as domestic or imported beers. They also have wine and homemade sangria by the pitcher or glass.

El Siboney lunch has specials seven days a week so be sure to check their online menu to find that day's special dish. Make sure to save room for dessert because they have Key Lime Pie, Natilla, Rice Pudding, Flan, and Mango/Guava Cheese Cake.

Key West

CUBAN CRIME
OF CAFFEINE

Cuban refugees seeking a new life in the United States braved the Florida Straits in this chug pictured in front of the Mel Fisher Museum. Photo by Mark Lee.

CUBAN CRIME OF CAFFEINE

There's really no crime going on here, it just gave me a chance to make a small Jimmy Buffett song reference, well kind of. The only crime in this case would be if you didn't get to try a cup of Cuban Coffee while you're in Key West. Due to its close proximity, located just 90 miles to the South across the Florida Straits, Cuba and Key West have had a long relationship sharing common interests, economical as well as cultural. Since the early 1830s, Cuban families have come to Key West and settled. Cuban cigars are known to be the finest in the world and in 1831 the first cigar factory opened in Key West. This provided steady work and income to its workers which further attracted many Cuban families who were well experienced in this industry. These families left their homeland seeking prosperity and political freedom from Spain and in doing so brought their customs, food, and culture with them.

Coffee is a big part of their lifestyle and Cuban coffee is very distinctive with a bold and delicious flavor. Many of Key West's citizens start their daily life with a sip of this energy in a cup in the small Cuban coffee shops and markets in town. I have had the chance to sample the wares of all of the vendors that I will tell you about in this chapter and have found them to be all delectable. You really can't go wrong with any of the places that I will highlight so just pick one and give it a try.

CUBAN COFFEE QUEEN

284 Margaret Street
Key West, FL 33040
Phone: (305) 292-4747
Open daily • 6:30 a.m.–7 p.m.
www.cubancoffeequeen.com

When I start my mornings off at the Cuban Coffee Queen at the Historic Seaport of Key West I'm already miles ahead of my usual routine as I am indulging two of my favorite passions. First, of course, I'm in Key West so, I mean who has a bad day in Key West? Second, is that I'm around the waterfront, surrounded by the many sailboats and yachts that are moored in the marina. This is where the day of the local charter boat captains start by preparing the boats to take tourists and sportsman out on the sea in search of wily game fish. Some of these boats are live aboards, some are used in the tourist trade giving waterfront tours of Key West, and still others are privately owned pleasure craft awaiting their next high seas adventure. I love to be around the water and especially the ocean. I find it is one of the best places for me to relax, reflect, and recharge. I like to get down to the waterfront early, before all of the hustle and bustle starts. Before all of the delivery trucks start servicing all of the cool waterfront restaurants such as The Half Shell Raw Bar, Waterfront Brewery, and The Schooner Wharf.

The barista this particular morning gave me a friendly greeting as he took my order for a large coffee and inquired if I was also having food. As I shuffled around in the courtyard of the Cuban Coffee Queen after having received my order, I breathed in the warm salty summer air. I sipped from my cup of coffee and was struck by the rich, bold flavor of this brew compared to my usual coffee back at home. As I sat on the bench just a few feet away from the order window of this Key West landmark, I saw the waterfront come to life and activity increase as the sun continued to rise.

Although I didn't get breakfast this morning, as I have other times, the menu is outstanding and the food is always tasty and made to order. They serve breakfast and lunch daily and are open from 6:30a.m. till sunset.

70

Breakfast consists of a large selection of sandwiches most of which are a combination of egg and cheese with a choice of with or without a meat such as ham, bacon, turkey, chorizo, or pork served on pressed Cuban bread. You'll also find cheese toast, buttered Cuban bread, and Cuban bagels available. If that's not to your liking they also have Guava and cream cheese on pressed Cuban bread. On the sweeter side they have strawberry and cheese or chocolate croissants.

Of course, they also have a variety of coffees such as café con leche, various size espressos, a Cuban Frappe, iced coffees, flavored coffees, and American coffee.

Order your coffee and breakfast sandwiches here at the Key West Seaport location. Photo credit by Mark Lee.

5 Brothers Grocery and Sandwich Shop

930 Southard Street
Key West, FL 33040
305-296-5205
Monday thru Saturday 6:00 a.m. – 3 p.m.
Closed Sunday
www.5brotherskeywest.com

Walk into the corner entrance of this Southard Street market and you're instantly surrounded by the aroma of strong coffee and delicious breakfast foods. Key Westers congregate inside and out of this Old Town neighborhood gathering place six mornings a week catching up on the local news and sipping Cuban café con leche and espresso from small Styrofoam cups. This is exactly what I encountered on the Wednesday morning that I strolled in and got more than I bargained for as I ordered the large Cuban coffee and a bacon and cheese sandwich on toasted Cuban bread. The coffee although pale brown due to the milk and sweet from the generous amount of sugar dissolved in the contents of this large white cup, still carried a powerful punch. What I didn't know when I ordered it was that the large café con leche was made with 4, yes 4 shots, of espresso with milk and sugar to taste. Without a doubt I was drinking all the supplemental energy that I would need to carry me on the long drive back up the Florida Keys to catch my afternoon flight in Miami. By the time I had arrived at Bahia Honda to take a few roadside pictures I nearly had enough energy to leap across the missing expanse of bridge where the old Overseas Highway used to meet land.

Although this market has been in existence for more than 70 years it wasn't until 1978 that a Cuban immigrant by the name of Heriberto Paez added coffee and food to the mix when he took over the business. Today his son, Pepe, brews coffee and greets the customers. They offer such breakfast delicacies as guava pastries, ham croquettes, cinnamon rolls, and more. They also make freshly prepared breakfast sandwiches on a Cuban roll in many combinations of cheese, sausage, bacon, ham, or egg.

Breakfast isn't the only meal of the day, they have different lunch specials depending on the day of the week. You can order such favorites as ropa vieja, picadillo and black beans, and chicken fricassee and garbanzo beans. All of the lunch specials are served with white rice, plantains, or yuca. They also offer an assortment of lunch sandwiches such as Cuban mix, hamburgers, pork, fish, or chicken. Sides of fries, plantains, or conch fritters are also on the menu.

The prices are very reasonable and the portions are plentiful so bring an appetite.

Morning gathering place for great coffee and breakfast in Old Town Key West. Photo credit by Mark Lee.

ANA'S CUBAN CAFÉ

1330 Simonton Street
Key West, FL 33040
(305)-296-4707

What may look like just another convenience store or neighborhood market on the outside is also serving some tasty Cuban food and coffee at the corner of South and Simonton Streets. Our first exposure to Ana's was actually one morning when my wife was looking for a tooth brush. Noticing that it also doubled as the Southernmost Market and Deli, we decided to take a look inside. Judging by the forming crowd outside we could tell that Ana's must have something good besides tooth brushes and sunscreen.

We found out that they start serving breakfast at 7 a.m. daily and offer good food at a fair price. You can also take your food and dine at one of the tables outside on their canopy covered porch. If you stayed on Duval till closing time which for many places is around 4 am you may opt for the Hangover Special. It comes with two eggs, bacon, ham, or sausage, home fries, Cuban toast, and coffee. I found this glowing review about Ana's, "The Hangover Breakfast saves lives and is a great deal for how much food you get!" Well, what else could you ask for? The Cuban coffee comes highly recommended as a strong eye opener and very tasty. They also prepare a variety of breakfast sandwiches and omelets. If you're in the mood for something fresh and fruity, try one of their smoothies made with fresh fruits such as watermelon, papaya, pineapple, strawberries, mango, or several others. They also have a fresh fruit bowl. Of course, they have a lot of coffee drink choices both Cuban and American.

Ana's also serves lunch and dinner and keeps on serving until 10 p.m. . They serve a variety of lunch and dinner platters which consist of a meat choice with side dishes of rice, beans, and plantains. The list includes Cuban roast pork, Picadillo, and Ropa Vieja just to name a few. They also prepare a few seafood dishes such as grouper fillet, breaded shrimp, and king fish. Sandwiches are also popular and they have a lot to choose from. You can order a Cuban sandwich, media noche, hamburger, hot dog, or many others. You can also get different sides to go with your meal like French Fries, tostones, croquettas, papa rellena, or chicken soup.

Why not top it off with some yummy dessert such as Key Lime Pie, Peanut Butter Brownie, or Bread Pudding. And there you have it. Before you know it you've just prepared for a big night out on the town and are ready to explore a whole new set of bars in Old Town Key West.

Ana's is located a few blocks from the Southernmost Point. Photo credit by Mark Lee.

THE BEST COFFEE IN TOWN

1222 White Street
Key West, FL
(305) 246-1666
Open Daily 4:00 a.m. – 5:00 p.m.
www.thebestcoffeeintown.net

With a name like that you better be able to deliver the goods and they do. I won't say if theirs actually is the best coffee in town, but it is certainly right up there. They also make a mean ham and cheese breakfast sandwich on Cuban bread. When you first drive up to this walk up food spot on White Street surrounded by the coin op laundry you may not be convinced, but let me tell you they know what they're doing.

They're menu is very similar to the competition down the street and is prepared hot and fresh to order. The menu has all of the breakfast sandwiches that you may be looking for. They have Cuban toast, cheese bread, egg and cheese, and either ham, bacon, or sausage with egg and cheese. They also have pastries and muffins if you want something a little lighter for breakfast. Their coffee is very good and you can order Café' con Leche, Colada, or half Colada. Their sandwiches and coffee were quite large and it was almost more than I could enjoy, but somehow, I managed to finish it. It was a lot of sandwich for $4.50.

The lunch menu is also very good with popular choices such as the Cuban mix, or a Steak, Chicken, Pork, or Turkey Sandwich. They also offer a Tuna or Chicken Salad sandwich. Looking for something a little more substantial, then you may want to order the four Mexican taco combo with soda or the Burrito or even the Cuban Tamales.

Their beverage choices, in addition to the coffee, consist of sodas, Goya juices, Red Bull, Yoo Hoo, Gatorade, and several more. I don't think you'll be disappointed by the Best Coffee in Town, but I'll let you decide if it actually is, "The Best Coffee in Town."

SANDY'S

1026 White Street
Key West, FL 33040
(305) 295-0159
Monday thru Wednesday: 5 a.m. TO 12 a.m.
Thursday: 5 a.m. – OPEN
Friday & Saturday: Open 24 hours
Sunday: Open to 12 a.m.
www.kwsandyscafe.com

My wife and I were out rambling in Key West one Thursday night, looking for something to eat and stumbled upon this really cool walk up restaurant that has the best Cuban sandwiches and café con leche. We had just finished watching a great Jimmy Buffet concert over at the Casa Marina with a few thousand other Parrot Heads and were starving from a day of travel south to make this event and skipping lunch in the process. We love Cuban sandwiches so much that we often have them at home.

It was with great delight that we found this barely hidden locals spot a mere stone's throw off Truman Avenue down White Street. They're open 24 hours a day, seven days a week so you can always get your fix for a Cuban mix and fries here. What is a Cuban mix you say? Well that's the same thing we said, a little bleary eyed as we peered towards the menu. As we read on we found that a Cuban mix sandwich has all of the traditional items found on a Cuban sandwich such as ham, roasted pork, Swiss cheese, and dill pickles on Cuban bread dressed with mustard. However, in Key West it gets kicked up a notch as their Cuban also has salami. I told one of the employees that when I've had Cuban sandwiches in Miami, I had never seen salami and he told me that you only see this in Key West. What a great addition to an already tasty sandwich. This isn't all that they offer as they have a full menu served all day, all night, and all the time. They offer breakfast platters and authentic Cuban coffee as well as breakfast wraps, lunch, and dinner platters, Mexican tacos, burritos, quesadillas, and sandwiches. Sandy's also has salads, soups, sides, and desserts. Every weekday you can have the special which can be anything from Ropa Vieja to Chicken Fricassee or BBQ Ribs. The daily special is served with rice, black beans, plantains, and bread.

You can also run into some of the nicest people. We bumped into some our friends from Chicago that also had been at the concert and we shared a seat at the lunch counter and talked about some of the other Buffet concerts that we had been too. One of our friends had recently seen Jimmy at La Cigale in Paris, France a few months back. After our late night snack we even gave them a ride back to Duval Street where we went our separate ways. Sandy's was a great ending to a memorable day, but we were pooped and ready to catch a nap before the next day's events.

Sandy's is not you tourist type flashy kind of place. The M&M coin operated laundry is in the same building to the rear of the restaurant. Sandy's is the real deal where you'll find a constant flow of real Key West people enjoying a fresh meal made to order.

Sandy's is our go to for a great Cuban Mix sandwich but they also have coffee. Photo credit by Mark Lee.

Key West

PLACES TO CRASH

This was a stormy day at the White Street Pier as a tropical storm passed just to the West. Photo credit Mark Lee.

KEY WEST HOTELS

So, it's 4 a.m., the bar is closing, and you hear this, "You don't have to go home, but you can't stay here!" Let's hope you've thought ahead and have a great place lined up to stay. Surely you'll want to take a nap before you head out to the beach and spend another night on the town. Key West has a variety of properties ranging from quaint bed and breakfasts to waterfront resorts. In case you need some ideas check out this list of great homes away from home to choose from:

1. Southernmost House, 1400 Duval Street, Key West, FL 33040
    Phone: (305) 296-3141
    Website: www.southernmosthouse.com

2. Casa Marina, 1500 Reynolds Street, Key West, FL 33040
    Phone: (305) 296-3535, (888)-303-5717
    Website: www.casamarinaresort.com

3. Key West Bed and Breakfast, 415 William Street, Key West, FL 33040
    Phone: (305) 296-7274
    Website: www.keywestbandb.com

4. Southernmost on the Beach, 508 South Street, Key West, FL 33040
    Phone: (305) 296-5611, (888) 449-0633
    www.southernmostresorts.com/southernmost-on-the-beach

5. The Speakeasy Inn, 1117 Duval Street, Key West, FL
    Phone: (305) 296-2680
    Website: www.speakeasyinn.com

Key West Bed and Breakfast is a cool place to stay on William Street in the center of an Old Town residential neighborhood. Photo by Mark Lee.

The Southernmost House is a beautiful waterfront hotel on the Atlantic side of Key West. Photo by Mark Lee.

6. Eden House, 1015 Fleming Street, Key West, FL 33040
   Phone: (305) 296-6868, (800) 533-5397
   Website: www.edenhouse.com

7. Ocean Key Resort, Zero Duval Street, Key West, FL 33040
   Phone: (305) 296-7701, (800) 328-9815
   Website: www.oceankey.com

8. Southern Most Hotel, 1319 Duval Street, Key West, FL 33040
   Phone: (305) 296-6577, (800) 354-4455
   Website: www.southernmostresorts.com

9. Pier House Resort Hotel and Resort, 1 Duval Street, Key West, FL 33040
   Phone: (305) 296-4600, (800) 327-8340
   Website: www.pierhouse.com

The Marker Hotel is on the Historic Key West Seaport and is within walking distance to shopping as well as many bars and restaurants. Photo by Mark Lee.

10. Parrot Key Hotel and Resort, 2801 N Roosevelt Blvd, Key West, FL 33040
    Phone: (305) 809-2200, (877) 741-5868
    Website: www.parrotkeyresort.com

11. Margaritaville Key West Resort and Marina,
    245 Front Street, Key West, FL 33040, Phone: (305) 294-4000
    Website: www.margaritavillekeywestresort.com

12. Best Western Hibiscus, 1313 Simonton Street, Key West, FL 33040
    Phone: (305) 294-3763, (800) 972-5100

13. Hyatt Key West Resort & Spa, 601 Front Street, KeyWest,FL, 33040
    Phone: (305) 809-1234, (888) 591-1234
    Website: www.keywest.hyatt.com

14. Cypress House Key West, 601 Caroline Street, Key West, FL 33040
    Phone: (305) 294-6969, (800) 549-4430
    Website: www.historickeywestinns.com/the-inns/cypress-house

15. Key Lime Inn, 725 Truman Ave, Key West, FL 33040
    Phone: (305)294-5229, (800) 549-4430
    Website: www.historickeywestinns.com/the-inns/key-lime-inn

16. Orchid Key Inn, 1004 Duval Street, Key West, FL 33040
    Phone: (305)296-9915, (800) 845-8384
    Website: www.orchidkey.com

17. The Reach, 1435 Simonton Street, Key West, FL 33040
    Phone:(305) 296-5000, (888)-318-4316
    Website: www.reachresort.com

18. Marquesa, 600 Fleming Street, Key West, FL 33040
    Phone: (305) 292-1919, (800) 869-4631
    Website: www.marquesa.com

19. Almond Tree Inn, 512 Truman Ave, Key West, FL 33040
    Phone: (305) 296-5415, (800) 311-4292
    Website: www.almondtreeinn.com

20. The Marker Waterfront Resort, 200 William Street, Key West, FL
    Phone: (305) 501-5193, (855) 485-9291
    Website: www.themarkerkeywest.com

21. The Inn at Key West, 3420 N. Roosevelt Blvd., Key West, FL
    Phone: (305) 297-5541, (866) 849-3753
    Website: www.theinnatkeywest.com

22. La Concha Hotel and Spa, 430 Duval Street, Key West, FL
    Phone: (305) 296-2991
    Website: www.laconchakeywest.com

23. 24 North Hotel, 3820 N. Roosevelt Blvd., Key West, FL
    Phone: (305) 320-0940
    Website: www.24northhotel.com

24. Santa Marina Suites, 1401 Simonton Street, Key West, FL 33040
    Phone: (305) 296-5678, (866) 726-8259
    Website: www.santamariasuites.com

25. Curry Mansion Inn, 511 Caroline Street, Key West, FL 33040
    Phone: (305)294-5349, (800)253-3466
    Website: www.currymansion.com

Originally built by Henry Flagler in the early 1900's, the Casa Marina is an oceanfront hotel that is part of the Waldorf chain. It provides luxury accommodations with beach area and two pools. Photo by Mark Lee.

STOCK ISLAND HOTELS

1. The Perry Hotel-Key West, 7001 Shrimp Rd., Stock Island Marina, Key West, FL
    Phone: (305) 296-1717
    Website: www.perrykeywest.com

2. Ocean's Edge Hotel and Marina, 5950 Peninsular Ave., Key West, FL
    Phone (305) 809-8204
    Website: www.oceansedgekeywest.com

Key West

TOURS AND ATTRACTIONS

TOURS AND ATTRACTIONS

There's plenty of history in Key West to be learned if you have the time and inclination. There are some excellent organized tours and lots of attractions. There are ghost tours, bar tours, and history tours... even some that combine a little of all of these elements. In this chapter we'll take a look at some of the established tours that are available in Key West. I'll also highlight some of the most popular attractions and let you know a few things about each one that might help you decide if you would like to go and check them out a little further.

The Conch Train is one of the best ways to see Key West and find out a little more. Photo courtesy of Historic Tours of America.

KEY WEST GHOST HUNT

305-395-1435
Tours depart nightly rain or shine
www.hauntedkeywest.com

What do you get when you combine one of the most haunted cities in America with a one of a kind, interactive paranormal experience? You get The Key West Ghost Hunt, the brainchild of noted author, entrepreneur, and Key West resident David L. Sloan.

Sloan started the original Key West Ghost Tours after relocating to the island in 1996. Before he came to town, ghost tours were pretty much unheard of in the United States, and after experiencing such a tour in Scotland, David knew that he wanted to start just such a tour.

David can actually trace his interests in ghosts and the supernatural back to his childhood in Philadelphia where he would conduct his own ghost tours in several historic hotels that his grandfather managed. However, he credits his kindergarten teacher with really kindling the fires of his ghostly passion. He recounts that she would tell stories to the class about a Native American spirit that was haunting her house and he knew that he was really hooked the day that she brought in a photograph of him for the class to see.

When he first moved to town, David was attempting to start his research on the ghosts of Key West, but was meeting with little success until one fateful evening. He recalls that he was in his '84 Thunderbird when the ghost of a man in his mid-30s appeared in his car and encouraged him to "Go back to the library." He admits we was taken aback, but did as the apparition bid and indeed returned to the library where he found that his luck was about to change. It is there where he met a local historian, Tom Hambright, who directed him to an archive that was literally brimming with Key West's ghostly happenings. It was this research that Sloan did which served as the beginnings of his and Key West's first ghost tour. He would later sell this successful tour business and embark on authoring a series of books on ghosts and help to establish tours in other cities. His tours and books have been featured on numerous cable channels including The History Channel, Discovery Channel, and Travel Channel in the U.S. and also international outlets such as the BBC.

In 2013, he started the venture that we know today as The Key West Ghost Hunt, and it is a product of the extensive research that has been done to this date and continues to evolve as Sloan pursues his passion for research of the paranormal.

Always on the cutting edge of his field, Sloan has the latest in ghost hunting technology on the tour. Each participant gets to experience and use items such as electromagnetic field detectors, divining rods, and laser thermometers. The ghost hunt guide also brings along trigger objects such as EM Pumps, SB-7 Spirit Box, Pendulum Board, and other equipment. They encourage guests to download Ghost Radar or the M2 Ghost Hunter app on their phone to track spirits during the hunt. It is said that a ghostly presence can be felt by a sudden chill in the air, and temps in the 20s have been detected in balmy Key West as a ghost makes his presence known. When asked about a typical hunt, Sloan said that the fascinating stories and dark history are guaranteed. It is also common to encounter the paranormal in the form of cold chills, people being poked and touched, ghostly sounds, and on rare occasions, an apparition. Key West is a hotbed of ghostly activity and is rife with stories of ghostly encounters in locations on the island such as The Ernest Hemingway Home, the Key West Lighthouse, and The Porter Mansion, which now houses a bar known as The Porch. Stories abound at The Porch that the ghost of Dr. Porter still visits to this day to toss wine glasses about and produces dimes from thin air.

Since I first became acquainted with David Sloan a few years ago

91

his business has continued to grow and increase in popularity. He has also continued to prove that he is an innovator in his field and has added new tours and experiences that are now available. You can choose from two different fun and exciting tours: Sloan's Key West Ghost Hunt and The Infamous Hauntings Tour.

Your ghostly adventure on Sloan's Key West Ghost Hunt starts every night of the week with a 9:15 p.m. check-in at Kelly's Caribbean Bar, Grill, and Brewery at 301 Whitehead Street. From there the 90 minute walking tour of Key West's most haunted neighborhoods begins. The tour departs rain or shine so call to make your reservations and be prepared to be entertained and amazed.

The Infamous Hauntings Tour meets at 7:15 p.m. at Gone Fishin! at 1102 Duval Street, and takes in some of Key West's "most infamous and iconic hauntings." This tour will amaze you with haunted tales involving Ernest Hemingway, The Haunted Lighthouse, Typhoid Mary, a Murdered Klansman, and more.

Your good time on Sloan's tours are guaranteed and I'll also give you a tip straight from Dave himself. If you book online you can save $5 by entering the code, SPECTER13, at checkout. Good luck and good hunting!

David Sloan and guest during a ghost hunt in Key West. Photo courtesy of Key West Ghost Hunt.

CONCH TRAIN TOUR

303 Front Street
1-888-916-8687 (TOUR)
www.conchtourtrain.com

What began as a family business in the 1958 has grown into a Key West tradition and remains one of the most famous attractions in the state of Florida to this day. It's also one of the best ways to see the island and learn about its colorful history and characters. Their friendly and knowledgeable staff have delighted and entertained over 15 million visitors during its many years of operation.

Its world famous black locomotives and yellow train cars can be seen crawling through Key West daily with new tours departing every thirty minutes. The first tour of the day starts at 9:30 a.m. and the last one leaves at 4:30 p.m. These ninety minute tours are fun and educational and you'll hear about some of Key West's famous former residents such as Ernest Hemingway, Mel Fisher, Jimmy Buffet, Tennessee Williams, and President Harry S. Truman. Of course you'll also learn about Henry Flagler, the visionary who built the engineering masterpiece called the Overseas Railroad which was the first completed in 1912 and connected the Florida mainland with the Keys before bridges were built for car travel to Key West.

The best way to catch the train is to head to the Front Street station, purchase your ticket, and board the train, but you can also climb on at Flagler Station or Truval Village if seats are available. It makes several stops along the way which give the opportunity to get refreshments, go to the restroom, and do a little shopping. The tour encompasses many sites of interest such as the Hemingway Home and Museum, the Key West Lighthouse, Truman's Little White House, and the Southernmost Point.

Having taken the tour myself, I can honestly say that this tour is one of the best ways to learn about the island and kind of get the lay of the land when you get to town. However, don't just take my word for it. I heard Jimmy Buffett himself say one of the first things he did when he got to town in 1972 was take the Conch Train Tour. With that kind of recommendation, what are you waiting for? Buy your ticket and get ready to board!

281 Front Street
Key West, Florida 33040
(305) 295-6616
www.kwahs.org

The Key West Art and Historical Society is dedicated to preserving the cultural heritage of the Florida Keys. It does this through the conservation of the island's historic structures and the collection of artifacts and art that reflect the history of the Conch Republic. It took a sharp witted and determined person to survive the tough lifestyle of this island nation in its early days. This is long before Henry Flagler's railroad came to town and forever changed the method of transport from mainland to island and even island to island. Through the museums vast collection of artifacts the history, determination, and creativity of the people of the Florida Keys can be seen in various displays throughout its three facilities. These three facilities are the Customs House, The Lighthouse and Keepers Cottage, and Fort East Martello.

The Key West Art and Historical Society actually came into being as a non-profit organization in 1949 and its first effort was to restore and preserve Fort East Martello as the first museum in the Florida Keys.

In the late 1960s the Lighthouse and Keeper's Quarters were acquired and a series of restorative projects took place in the 1980s which transformed the Keepers Cottage from a former military museum into more of what of you see today. Today it gives a glimpse into the life of the dedicated people who kept the light burning in the lighthouse as a safety beacon to the ships at sea. The Keeper's Cottage contains period furniture, artifacts, and pictures which give us a peek into the way of life and times of early Key West. The Customs House with its impressive scale and outdoor figures is stands bold on the Key West waterfront. It was originally built in 1891 in the Richardsonian Romanesque and architectural style and served as Key West's customs office, postal service, and district courts. Later it served as the headquarters of the Caribbean and Gulf of

Mexico operations of the US Navy. After it was declared surplus by the Navy and sat idle for almost twenty years, it was finally acquired by the state of Florida in 1991. It was at this time that the state of Florida leased the Customs House to the Key West Art and Historical Society to be used as a museum. As you walk down Front Street approaching the building you can't help but notice it as this massive four story brick structure looms in front of you. You can also see two people, larger than life and in full color, kissing outside the museum. This is a work entitled Embracing Brace and was inspired by the iconic photo on the couple kissing in Time Square after WW II is over.

The museum has rotating exhibitions as well as permanent displays. Some of the permanent displays, including the art of Tennessee Williams and others, provide a glimpse into Henry Flagler's Overseas Railway, Stanley Papio and Ernest Hemingway's lives. To find out more about the Key West Art and Historical Society and what it has to offer, check it out on their website and be sure to visit.

Key West Art and Historical Society's Custom House Museum. Photo by Mark Lee.

EAST MARTELLO MUSEUM

3601 South Roosevelt Blvd.
(305) 296-3913
Open Daily 9:30 a.m. to 4:30 p.m.

I had passed by this Civil War era brick fort many times before, but had never gone in until recently. I had heard about this large stuffed doll with mysterious powers that resided within its walls. I had even read David Sloan's book about this Robert the Doll when it came out a few years ago, and also purchased a miniature replica of this famous Key West resident. However, it took me a little while to work up enough courage to go see him on his home turf, The East Martello Fort and Museum.

If you're not familiar with Robert, he was the childhood toy of Gene Otto and as legend has it this stuffed doll has the ability to move around as well as cast any number of bad luck, evil spells, or what have you if you anger him. Knowing that Sloan, local author and business-man, had taken Robert out for a rare visit to Islamorada for a lecture and was now back, I thought this might be the perfect time to stop in and say hello. I also wanted to get a picture for my book, but as you that have read Sloan's book about Robert know this is not a simple process. More about that later.

Construction of East Martello was originally started in 1862 and it was intended to be a fortress that safeguarded Key West's southern wa-ters against attack by the Navy of the Confederate States. Although Key West was under Union control most of the citizens of Key West sided with the Confederacy. Various factors helped slow the construction and delay completion of the project. During the summers months, the swel-tering heat and humidity coupled with the yellow fever outbreaks took its toll on the workforce. A devastating hurricane destroyed parts of the fort in 1864 and finally in 1865 work halted leaving the fort construction incomplete. During the Spanish American War, World Wars I, and World Wars II the fort was used as a radio post, storage, and soldiers' barracks. It sat neglected and mostly untouched after World War II until the Key West Art and Historical Society in 1950 sought to resurrect it and turn it into its first museum. Work began in 1959 and the fortress was restored to a useable state and opened in February 1951 as the Key West Museum.

The East Martello Museum gives a glimpse into the beginnings of Key West all the way back to the heritage of its first Native American inhabitants, the Calusa Indians, and traces a pathway through to modern times. There are exhibits recalling the Wrecking Days, Sponging and fishing, Cigar Manufacturing, and the integral influences of the Cuban people on the Southernmost City. It also houses works of art featuring the famous folk artist Stanley Papio. Papio was a welder by trade and would encourage people to leave their old cars and appliances on his land. He would use this "junk" and transform it into a work of art with his metal working and welding skills. In Key West, every May, there is a celebration of his work and influences called the Papio Kinetic Parade. It is made up of mobile works of art and bicycles which are all propelled with human power. Oh yeah, back to Robert. When I entered the museum, and walked up the steps I told the staff that I was there working on my book and wanted to see Robert and get a picture. She said that would be fine and pointed me in the right direction with one final warning.... make sure you ask Robert's permission. This may seem a strange request you say, but one that I was sure to comply with. Evidently, Robert does not like to have his picture taken without first being asked permission. There is a long history of people that have not given Robert the respect that he is due. When this happens they usually meet with some unpleasant consequences such as missed flights, flat tires, and broken cameras and cell phones. As I was walking down the breezeway, I spied Robert a distance down the hall in his own room. It was dimly lit, but I could make out that it was him. The moment I saw him I must admit there was a little apprehension as the hairs rose up on the back of my neck and I also felt a little chill. I got ahold of myself and thought that this was silly, a grown man stressed out by a giant stuffed children's toy. I guess my own childhood memories of the movie Poltergeist, in which a menacing toy clown attacks one of the main stars of the movie, were getting to me. As I moved closer and finally came face to face with Robert I was about to snap a photo as my wife stopped me. She implored me to first ask his permission. I felt a little silly, but at the time we were the only ones in the area so I blurted out these words, "Robert, can I please take your picture?" Hearing no response, I snapped away. After I had finished I was sure to also say thank you. There are quite a few letters posted around his Lucite cube home from people who were not thought to be polite to Robert and who had all met with some unpleasant circumstance. The most recent that comes to mind was a nationally renowned Ghost Hunt documentary that aired last year. During the show one of the participants had been rude to Robert and I remember hearing that after the taping he had a stroke. That was all I needed to hear and should be all you need to hear too. If you should visit Robert in the East Martello Museum please be polite. I would hate to be hearing about any of you being affected by the curse of Robert the Doll.

Also, you'll want to be sure to see the sculpture garden that lies protected in the walls of the courtyard of the museum. It makes for a nice walk and some interesting scenery. You'll find the museum adjacent to the Key West Airport on South Roosevelt Street, which interestingly enough according to one of my friends is the only stretch of Highway A1A that you'll find in the Keys. The rest is US 1.

Fort East Martello Museum, home of Robert the Doll. Photo by Mark Lee

The art of Stanley Papio, who turned junk into masterpieces. Photo by Mark Lee.

Various works of Stanley Papio. Note the "Bowlegged Bride" in the background. Photo credit Mark Lee.

One of Key West's most famous residents, Robert the Doll. Photo by Mark Lee.

KEY WEST LIGHTHOUSE AND KEEPERS QUARTERS

938 Whitehead Street
Key West, Florida 33040
(305) 294-0012
www.kwahs.org/museums/lighthouse-keepers-
quarters/history

The present Key West Lighthouse has stood since the mid 1800s as a sentinel and navigational aide to the sailors at sea to assist in providing safe travel.

In 1887 the Keepers Quarters were added to the grounds to give modern housing facilities to the lighthouse keepers as well as their families. The light in this structure continued to burn until December of 1969. At this time, due to modern navigational aids and methods, it was obsolete and turned off. Previously the Keepers Cottage was turned into a military museum which is how it stayed until 1980s when it underwent a three-year restoration process. During this time it was decided to return the cottage to its original state and provide visitors to the lighthouse with a real look at the life of a lighthouse keeper and his family.

The little clapboard house was stocked with historic furniture, artifacts, and photographs of the culture and history of early Key West.This museum is open daily year round and has one of the best views in town. It is located across the street from the Hemingway House.

This Royal Poinciana tree shows fiery red blooms on the grounds of the Key West Lighthouse. Photo by Mark Lee.

HARRY S. TRUMAN

Little White House
111 Front Street
(305) 294-9911
www.trumanlittlewhitehouse.com

What started out as a short term stay to recuperate in the warm and sunny climate of Key West turned out to be a lifelong love of the town and The Little White House. In fact he liked it so much that President Truman told his wife, Bess, " I've a notion to move the capital to Key West and just stay."

The Little White House in Key West served as the winter office for President Harry S. Truman, and he spent a total of 175 days there during his time in office. He was the 33rd President of the United States and had been serving as the Vice President until the unexpected death of President Franklin D. Roosevelt. Truman came to power in a turbulent time as World War II was still raging in the Pacific with Japan. His Presidency was marked by some important issues including the use of the Atomic Bomb to end the World War, the rebuilding of Europe after the war, the formation of NATO, and civil rights at home. While in office, President Truman made a total of eleven visits to The Little White House. While in Key West the President used the Little White House as his second headquarters and ran the government, hosted important meetings, and carried on the affairs of his office from there. In the archives there are detailed logs of his visits including the important people that joined and met with him on his trips.

The Little White House has stood since 1890 and for most of its existence it was part of the U.S. Naval installation in Key West. However in 1974, the submarine base was closed and the Little White House went unused for a period of 12 years. In 1987, the ownership of the Little White House was transferred to the State of Florida. It has gone through extensive renovations since changing ownership with great care taken to return it to its 1949 appearance. The majority of the furnishings that you see today are original.

Although it is most closely associated with President Truman there have been five other active or former US Presidents to visit including, Taft, Eisenhower, Kennedy, Carter, and Clinton. Every year over 100,000 people visit the Little White House and it is Florida's only Presidential site.

KEY WEST SHIPWRECK MUSEUM

1 Whitehead Street
305-292-8990
Open Daily 9:40 a.m. to 5:00 p.m.
www.keywestshipwreck.com

This museum gives an interesting look at what it might have been like to have been in Key West in the 1850s when wrecking was the biggest industry in town. During this time more than 100 ships a day passed near Key West which was reputed to have some of the most treacherous waters around. Indeed at least one ship per week would get entangled in the Florida reef and need rescue.

It was the wreckers who would brave dangerous conditions to perform the rescue of crew and cargo. The first person to reach the ship would be named wrecking master and would control the salvage of the ship as well as get a larger payout. The valuable cargo from the ship would be auctioned later and the courts had authority over deciding how much compensation was due the wreckers. Depending upon the danger of the job and time spent on site, the reward paid to the wreckers could range from 25 to 50 percent of the profit from the auctioned goods.

The Key West ShipWreck Museum uses an interesting mix of actors, films, and artifacts from real wrecks to show you how this industry made Key West one of the richest cities in the United States in the 1800s. Many of the fine homes that you see today were the former residences of the wreckers of Key West. Asa Tift who built what is known as the Hemingway House on Whitehead Street was a big part of the town's wrecking industry. William Curry was also a master wrecker and became Florida's first millionaire and settled on Caroline Street where you see the beautiful Curry Mansion Inn.

If you buy your tickets online you can save about 10 percent or you can buy a combination ticket and see both the Key West Aquarium and the Shipwreck Museum to save even more.

The Key West Shipwreck Treasures museum looms large with its observation towers in the background. Photo by Mark Lee.

KEY WEST AQUARIUM

1 Whitehead Street
888-544-5927
Daily. 10 a.m. to 6 p.m. – 365 days a year.
Tours offered every half hour starting at 10:00 a.m. through
5:00 p.m.
www.keywestaquarium.com

The Key West Aquarium is the only public aquarium in Key West and has been open since 1935. It is located at the corner of Front and Whitehead Street on "world famous" Mallory Square and is one of the most popular attractions in town. The Key West Aquarium gives visitors an up close look at sharks, turtles, stingrays, and tropical fish that are native to the waters of Key West and also is active in the conservation of the delicate eco-system of the Florida Keys.

The Key West Aquarium is a product of the Great Depression and was built as a project of the Works Project Administration. During the Depression the town of Key West was broke and had asked the Federal government for assistance. The government thought that the island community of Key West would make a great tourist attraction so they sent the WPA to town to build the aquarium and other attractions. This would provide much needed construction jobs for the locals while it was being built and then afterward help generate tourist activity which would further stimulate the economy.

The aquarium offers guided tours and feedings that last 30 to 40 minutes as you walk thru and view the various parts of the facility. During the tours the guide feeds the marine life all the while educating the participants with information about the aquarium and Key West. The tours start with an intro to the Touch Tank and then you are given a chance to hand feed stingrays, touch a shark's tails, and see other creatures. An extra benefit of purchasing a ticket to the tour is that each ticket is good for two consecutive days, so if you don't see it all the first time you can come back the next day and do it all over again. Another money saving tip: buy your tickets before arriving on the website and save ten percent!

Key West First Legal Rum Distillery

105 Simonton Street,
Key West, FL 33040
(305) 294-1441
Monday – Saturday 10:00 a.m. – 8:00 p.m.
Sunday 10:00 a.m. – 6:00 p.m.
www.keywestlegalrum.com

TOURS:
Monday – Friday 1:00 p.m. and 3:00 p.m. & 5:00 p.m. Happy Hour Tour!
Saturday 1:00 p.m. and 3:00 p.m.

You'll find Key West Legal Rum Distillery on Simonton Street in Old Town Key West. It is, as its name says, the first Legal rum maker in Key West. Part of its name "Legal Rum" harkens back to the prohibition days when rum running to Cuba and moonshining was the only way to get a drink of rum in the Keys.

Key West Legal Rum was opened in 2013 by multi-talented entrepreneur, Chef Paul Menta. However, to label him just a chef would not do him justice. He is an entrepreneur, distiller, as well as a record holding kite surfer. He actually holds the record for the fastest time for kite surfing from Key West to Cuba.

Chef Menta hails from Philadelphia where he grew up cooking with his grandmother and later graduated from culinary school. After school he went to Europe to further hone his craft with some of the best chefs in France and Spain. Just prior to relocating to Key West in 1984, he also spent time in Latin America where he refined his philosophy of using local products to make the best possible dishes. It is this technique that he uses in his Simonton Street distillery. Chef Menta uses only the best locally sourced products to make his unique Key West Legal Rum. He uses Florida produced Demerara sugar as the base of his rums instead of molasses and uses locally sourced fruits and products to flavor his unique spirits. He also does one other thing that no other rum maker in the world does. He takes his natural oak wood barrels down to beach where he fills them with sea water. After the barrels swell he empties out the water and uses the salt cured, charred barrels to give his rum its final color and character.

As you tour the distillery you see on the walls around you pictures and reminders of Key West's sometimes not so legal forays into the liquor business.

There are mugshots and artifacts from the Prohibition days which help to pay homage to those Key Westers that ran rum when it was illegal to do so.

When you tour the facility there will be a chance to taste the product and also an opportunity to purchase some of their delicious hand crafted rums. The Key West Legal Rum Distillery is a highly recommended stop and if you buy a shot glass you get to sample all of their rums. The staff here is great and does a great job of making you feel welcome.

If you see Chef Paul ask him about his recent Rum Running experiences. He just checked off one of his bucket list items by being the first person to take a bottle of Key West made rum to Cuba. He's proud of his accomplishment and I'm sure he has some interesting stories from his great trip.

Lots of fun to be had out on the water in the Florida Keys. Photo by Mark Lee.

TOP TEN KEY WEST TO DO LIST

1. **Picture at the Southernmost Point**: Erected by the city of Key West in 1983, nearly a million tourists per year have their picture taken at the Southernmost Point Buoy. Located at the corner of Whitehead and South streets, it is considered to be the Southernmost Point in the USA. If you're feeling adventurous jump in and start swimming for Cuba. It's only 90 miles from here.
   Corner of Whitehead and South Streets,
   www.southernmostpointusa.com

2. **Hemingway House:** Found just down the street from the Southernmost Point at 907 Whitehead Street this was the home of Ernest Hemingway in the 1930s. The home was originally constructed in 1851 by Asa Tift from Georgia who was a marine architect and salvage wrecker of the day. It was purchased and renovated by Ernest and Pauline Hemingway in 1931 and became home to them and their children. Hemingway took great pleasure in his years in Key West and spent his time writing, fishing on his boat, and drinking with his friends most afternoons at Sloppy Joe's.
   **907 Whitehead Street, (305) 294-1136,
   www.hemingwayhome.com**

Home of Ernest Hemingway. Photo by Mark Lee.

3. **Mel Fisher Maritime Museum:** If you want to know the definition of an optimist, you should see a picture of Mel Fisher in the dictionary. This larger than life man's motto was "Today's the day" as every day he and his crew would search for the treasure of the Atocha in the waters off the Florida Keys. The Atocha was a Spanish ship that sank in a

hurricane in 1622 laden with precious metals and gemstone that had been mined from Central and South America. For sixteen years, Mel Fisher and crew, including members of his family, searched unceasingly for these hidden treasures. Through pain and perseverance he finally found his quest and this museum stands as a monument to him and his indomitable spirit.

200 Greene Street, (305)294-2633, www.melfisher.org

The front of the Mel Fisher Maritime Museum. See treasure recovered from sunken Spanish ships and find out what all it took to recover these riches. Photo by Mark Lee.

4. **Key West Art and Historical Society:** The Key West Art and Historical Society maintains three sites which are The Custom House Museum, Fort East Martello, and The Lighthouse and Keeper's Quarters. The KWAHS functions to preserve the culture of the Florida Keys and exhibits artwork of all kinds that emanate from the region. They are also the caretakers of some of the personal items that belonged to Ernest Hemingway.

281 Front Street, (305) 295-6616, www.kwahs.org

Life like art of Seward Johnson around the KWAHS. Photo by Mark Lee.

5. **Kermits Key Lime Pies:** I think I make a pretty special Key Lime Pie but when you're in Key West you owe it to yourself to see Kermit for all things Key Lime. Kermit has been featured by Food Network, National Geographic, and even Paula Deen as having the best Key Lime Pie around. He doesn't stock just pies as he offers a variety of items made with Key Lime including cookies, salsa, jelly beans, and olive oil. He even has a super website to order his wares from once you're back home and craving a taste of lime.
   200 Elizabeth Street, (305) 296-0806, www.keylimeshop.com

It's none other than Kermit himself greeting customers at his Elizabeth Street location. One of the hardest working people I know. It's rare when I have not seen him outside year round greeting his customers with a pie and a smile! Photo by Stacye Lee.

6. **Key West Shipwreck Museum:** In the 1800s, wrecking was a major industry in Key West and the lifeblood of the community. When a shipwreck was announced in town the race was on to

work the salvage of the crew, ship, and cargo. This museum provides a peek into the past of Key West and a vital part of its history. **1 Whitehead Street, (305) 292-8990, www.keywestshipwreck.com**

7. **Conch Train Tour:** The Conch Train is a rolling tour through the streets of Key West and draws its heritage from Henry Flagler's Overseas Railroad. The Overseas Railroad was an extension of the Florida East Coast Railway and connected the Keys with the Florida mainland with daily passenger and freight train service from 1912 till 1935. The fun and informative Conch Train tour has been running since 1958 and takes in over 100 points of interest in Key West. Your friendly and knowledgeable "engineer" will regale you with tales of Key West past and present.
303 Front Street, (305) 294-5161, www.conchtourtrain.com

8. **Dry Tortugas National Park:** This beautiful and remote park can be found around 70 miles to the west of Key West. It is made up of seven small islands and is accessible only by boat or seaplane. Fort Jefferson, an 1800s era fortress, still stands here surrounded by stunning crystalclear waters. The all-inclusive tour on the Yankee Freedom III ferry which runs from Key West to the Dry Tortugas is an all-day event and includes a narrated tour of the fort, a chance to swim from the beach to the reef and breathtaking opportunities to snorkel and witness the abundant marine life.
(305) 242-7700, www.nps.gov/drto

9. **Key West Aquarium:** The Key West Aquarium is located on Mallory Square at 1 Whitehead Street. It is open year round and offers guided as well as self-guided tours. During these tours the staff will educate you about the marine life in the tanks as well as offer chances to hand feed the stingrays and sharks. One of the highlights of the exhibits is a chance to touch a live shark on the tail.
1 Whitehead Street, (305) 296-2051, www.keywestaquarium.com

10. **Sunset Celebration at Mallory Square:** The best way to end your day in Key West is to plan on celebrating at sunset at Mallory Square. Every day of the week, two hours before sunset the masses gather to witness the setting of the sun as it gently disappears into the Gulf. An eclectic collection of artists, street performers, psychics, and food vendors provide entertainment as well as tasty treats. The performers include sword swallowers, fire jugglers, and even cats walking tight ropes.

    Mallory Square, 305-292-7700, www.sunsetcelebration.org

Sailboats take a sunset cruise just off Mallory Square. Photo by Mark Lee.

Key West

GETTING LOCAL

GETTING LOCAL

As I said in my introduction, I like to wander away from Duval Street when I'm looking for things to do because I feel like that is where you start to meet the real Key West. Not to say that there aren't some great places on Duval to go, but I like to get off the tourist's path and meet the natives. That is the Conchs and the freshwater Conchs that own and run the businesses around town. After all Key West is more than a collection of bars. It's the people that make a town and the local businesses. It's there that I meet the people that sometimes work two and three jobs to afford to live in this island paradise. It's there where I hear about their personal stories of how they came to town and what makes Key West special to them. In this chapter I'll let you know where I go in town to get a little local color and see what makes Key West tick.

VOCABULARY LESSON:

Conch: Person born in the Florida Keys, an island chain at the southernmost tip of Florida, also referred to as the "Conch Republic."

Freshwater Conch: Anyone having lived in the Keys for seven or more consecutive years may call themselves a "freshwater conch."

PEPE'S

806 Caroline Street
Key West, FL 33040
(305) 294-7192
Open Daily 7:30 a.m. – 9:30 p.m.
Breakfast -7:20 a.m. – 12:00 p.m.
Lunch- Noon – 5:00 p.m.
Dinner 5:00 p.m. 9:30 p.m.
www.pepeskeywest.com

On a warm November Sunday morning as I came around the corner on my scooter and saw a parking lot filled with bright red Key West fire trucks it confirmed what I already knew, that I was in the right place for one of the best breakfasts in town. Pepe's is one of those locals places that you find every once in a while in the Keys. The kind of place where you can sit at a varnished wooden bar and watch a couple of friendly sun kissed bar maidens squeeze case after case of fresh Florida oranges into juice used to make tasty hand crafted concoctions such as a mimosa or screw driver. They also make a great Bloody Mary which is once again made from scratch with their own recipe. No mix used here.

They serve breakfast, lunch, and dinner and we liked it so much in fact we ate there two days in a row. Their menu is superb and we found everything that we had to be made from the freshest ingredients and prepared just as we had ordered.

The first morning there, we sat in the open air courtyard waiting on a table to open up breathing in the salty air mixed with the smell of fresh fried bacon, eggs, and strong Cuban coffee. Pepe's has their own blend of coffee which has a great aroma and plenty of bold flavor. We liked it so much in fact that we brought a couple of bags back home and were only disappointed when we had brewed the last cup which only left us wanting more. As we sat sipping our coffee on this sunny morn we were amused to see a mother hen and her baby chicks scurrying freely around the brick courtyard. This is Key West after all and chickens are everywhere.

When we saw two spots open at the bar top we took them. We had a couple of friendly bartenders to chat with and we learned a little more about local life as we made our decision of what to have for our meal and also received input as to their favorites. Next to us was a NASCAR marketing executive who works with one of the racing teams from our home state of Georgia. We chatted about the racing business and the upcoming race in Homestead the next week and found out about the in and the outs of the Chase. The Chase is series of post season racing events which ultimately determine who is the champion for the year and wins the NASCAR Sprint Cup. After a short while our meals had arrived and boy did they look great! I had scrambled eggs with cheese, bacon, home fried potatoes, and a bowl of grits. I also had the bread of the day which was tasty key lime. My wife had the creamed chipped beef on toast which she said was delicious. By the way, both dishes were considered strong medicine to prevent the onset of what my friend, Captain Marlin Scott, calls the Duval flu. It certainly made for a good start to our day and prepared us to see what's happening in Old Town Key West and furthermore another great concert at the Casa Marina later that night.

As I said earlier they have also have lunch and dinner which we plan on sampling on our next visit. The lunch menu is loaded with a variety of sandwiches and burgers. You have a choice of bread and macaroni salad, German fried potatoes, or fresh made cole slaw.

The dinner menu has a variety of oyster appetizers such as raw on the half shell, baked, Florentine, Mexican roasted, and Rudi style baked. They also soups and salads. For your entrée you can choose from a choice New York Strip, Ribeye, or Filet. They also have pork, chicken, and fresh fish dishes. All dinners are served with potato, fresh vegetable and house made cornbread.

Pepes is one of our favorite breakfast stops. Photo by Mark Lee.

Best seat in the house out at the courtyard bar. Photo by Mark Lee.

HOG FISH BAR AND GRILL

6810 Front Street
Stock Island, FL 33040
(305) 293-4041
Monday thru Saturday 11 a.m. – 11 p.m.
Sunday 8 a.m. – 11 p.m.
www.hogfishbar.com

This is Key West before the tourists came and you'll see what I'm talking about if you take the trouble to find this hidden gem in Safe Harbor Marina. You'll have to leave Key West proper and go across the Cow Key Chanel Bridge and down the road a bit veer right onto MacDonald Avenue. You'll take a right at FishbusterZ onto 4th Street then an almost immediate left onto Front Street and keep on going past a string of rusty mobile homes until you come to the Hog Fish which is a large open air thatched roof restaurant to the right on the working waterfront of Stock Island.

Bobby Mongelli and his wife Michelle have made this the place to be for the freshest seafood and a peak into what it must have been like to be in "Old Key West." If you made it here its no accident, you're either a local or had good directions. This is one of our go to places for tasty seafood and a place to relax. We like to get one of the wooden picnic tables on the right hand side of the restaurant and watch the boats. Last time we were there a few tables down some of the guests were hand feeding the tarpon looming just a few feet away in the clear green water.

You can't go wrong with any of their seafood. We like the Key West Pink Shrimp, Hog Fish Sandwich, and fish tacos.

GRUNTS

409 Caroline Street

I found this little gem on a Sunday evening not by accident, but quite on purpose. A couple of friends, Chris and Dani, were playing here with their band, the Shanty Hounds, and I wanted to go hear them and check the Key West music scene.

What a cool place this is and a great intimate setting to hear some good local music. Grunts is housed in a little cottage set back from the road with a quaint brick patio out front with tables and seating. You'll find it on the short side of Caroline Street running just west of Duval.

The little building that houses Grunts was once part of the Old Island Trading Post at Porter Docks, where the Pier House is now, and was moved and restored. Inside there are period signs and décor somewhat reminiscent of a waterfront Key West fishing tackle store. The beer is cold and they also have wine, but no liquor. Although Grunts does not have food, there is an excellent food trailer restaurant called Garbo's in the rear of the property. It has been featured on Food

Network show, *Diners Drive-Ins and Dives* and I hear its food is second to none. You'll see more about them in a later section.

Grunts feels like it's one of those out of the way local's places, but that's only partly true because it's literally a stone throw to either Whitehead Street in one direction and bustling Duval Street in the other. Locals like it because the prices are right and the beer selection is good and cold.

If you want to feel like a local for a night, try out Grunts. You'll find one of the cleanest and friendliest bars in town. They have live music many nights and you're almost guaranteed a front row bar stool.

Here is Grunts on Caroline Street. Note the new airstream food trailer behind it. Photo by Mark Lee.

SANDY'S

1026 White Street
Key West, FL 33040
(305) 295-0159
Monday thru Wednesday: 5 a.m. – 12 a.m.
Thursday: 5 a.m. – OPEN
Friday & Saturday: Open 24 hours
Sunday: Open to 12 a.m.
www.kwsandyscafe.com

This is the place where you'll find locals coming for their daily fix for breakfast, lunch, or dinner. In the morning you can get your Cuban coffee and your favorite breakfast sandwich, platter, wraps, or sweets. For lunch and dinner choose from platters, Cuban Mix, pork, fish, or ham and cheese sandwiches. They also have specials Monday thru Friday including Beef Stew, Ropa Vieja, Chicken Fricasse, BBQ Ribs, and Pepper Steak.

If Mexican food is more to your liking they also have tacos, burritos, sandwiches, and quesadillas. For the lighter appetite, they also offer a variety of soups and salads. For dessert they have Key Lime Pie, Rice Pudding, and Flan. Sandy's is the real thing!

THE CHART ROOM

1 Duval Street

(305) 296-4600

Daily 4:30 p.m. – 2:00 a.m.

Happy Hour 4:30 p.m. – 6:00 p.m.

Where else can you grab parched peanuts out of a real wooden barrel and also get free hot dogs and popcorn as long as you're buying drinks? This Key West institution surrounded by the Pier House Resort, has maintained its 1970s time warp as Key West developed around it. A visit to the island is not complete without a late night séance with the spirits of bartenders and patrons past. Rumored former clients of this urgent care for anything that ails you include Truman Capote, Tennessee Williams, Hunter S. Thompson, Bob Marley, Robin Williams, and Jim Croce.

Jimmy Buffett drank and played here and wrote a song about former bartender, the late Phil Clark called *A Pirate Looks at Forty*. If these walls could talk they would fill volumes with all that has gone on within its compact "hotel room" dimensions. In Key West's formative years in the 70s you could probably find more of the officials here than at City Hall.

As you sit at its rich mahogany bar, a picture of successful treasure hunter Mel Fisher stares down from above as well as others grinning from ear to ear. Another interesting feature of the bar is that the ashes of some of its most notable patrons have been encased in holes drilled into the bartop. There are albums of pictures in the back containing memories of years past. On one of my trips through here, I had just missed author and friend, Tom Corcoran, who is a former bartender at the Chart Room. It was Corcoran who served Jimmy Buffett his first beer in town and has remained friends with him to this day.

I highly recommend this as a stop on your Key West adventure. As the night wears on, the Chart Room really gets going. I even got a job offer my last time on the bar stool. What happened....I turned it down.

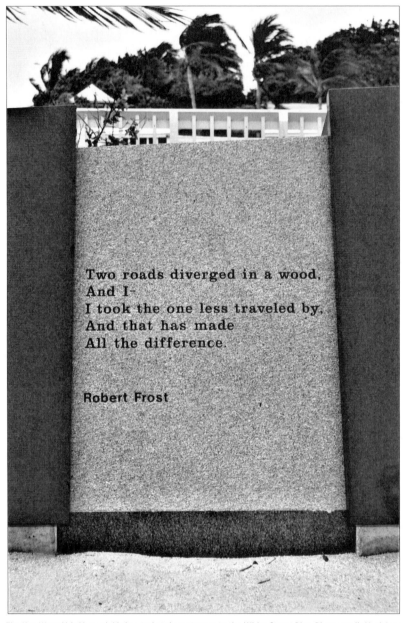

The Key West Aids Memorial is located at the entrance to the White Street Pier. Photo credit Mark Lee.

THE SUNSHINE GRILL

1110 White Street
Key West, Florida
305-294-8089
www.sunshinegrillkeywest.com

The Sunshine Grill is a cool diner with delicious food and great prices. Located a short five minute drive from busy Duval Street, you'll find a friendly and inviting staff serving a delicious assortment of dishes for breakfast, lunch, and dinner.

Owners Chris and Noelle Itrato are both from New England and met while doing character work after college at Disney World in Orlando. Chris was Goofy and Noelle was Mickey Mouse. The Itratos, both with a solid background in customer service from their Disney World days and fresh off a successful foray into the culinary world with the Moes Southwestern Grill brand in Alabama, decided to come back to sunny Florida and raise a family and pursue their dreams in Key West. Chris says, "It was kind of like Goofy and Mickey opened a restaurant" when they came to Key West. However having dined at their restaurants there's no funny business going on here. They cook up some of the tastiest food in a warm and inviting atmosphere and even if you're not a local you'll feel like one before you leave.

One of the things that struck me about the Grill is just how comfortable and familiar it was from the moment I entered the front door. Back where I'm from, we had a diner on the main street in town which served three meals a day. You could walk in about anytime of the day and find several folks that you know and the waitresses and staff treated you like family. That's the same vibe that I feel at the Sunshine Grill. They treat you like a regular whether it's your first time dining there or not.

The breakfast menu is available all day from open to close. It has the usual eggs any style served with toast and home fries or grits. Yes, they do have a good bowl of grits which means a lot to a Southern boy like me. They also serve great build your own omelets, pancakes, French toast, shrimp & grits, and lox with bagels. Chris says that the biscuits and gravy is one of their specialties on the breakfast menu and it's from the Chef's own secret recipe. Another special touch is that they try to use fresh fruit and vegetables that are locally grown and offered at the Key West Farmers market.

The lunch/dinner menu has an assortment of appetizers such as fried pickles, "super fattening" Sunshine fries smothered in cheese and bacon with ranch dressing, hummus dip, soup of the day, and home made chili and cornbread. For your entrée choose from their signature one half pound burger or foot long hot dog. They also have an assortment of mouthwatering sandwiches including one of their specialties, the Southern Deep Fried Chicken Sandwich.

If you saved room for dessert you won't be disappointed. They have The Sunshine Classic Banana Split, Strawberries, Bananas and Cream, Milkshake Madness, and an assortment of sundaes and ice cream in a cone or cup. They proudly serve Mattheessen's ice cream which is a locally produced homemade product. Last but not least, they have Key Lime Pie exceptionally made by Chef Mikey from scratch. It is after all Key West where Key Lime Pie is considered a staple of the dessert menu. By the way, Mikey also makes the tie-dyed t-shirts available for sale here at the Grille.

Chances are that you may see either Chris, Noelle or both working here as they both take shifts in the restaurant. They also have a new business called Paint a Piece in Paradise located a short walk down the street at 1120 White Street. Why don't you live like a local for a day and give them both a try.

The Sunshine Grill is also a cool breakfast destination. Tell Chris that I sent you. Photo by Mark Lee.

FAUSTO'S FOOD PALACE

522 Fleming Street
(305) 296-5663
Monday thru Saturday 7:30 a.m. – 8:00 p.m.
Sunday 7:30 a.m. – 7:00 p.m.
www.faustos.com

Before there was Winn Dixie and long before Publix there was Fausto's Food Palace, Key West's long time local grocer, where those in the know have been shopping for over ninety years. Fausto's was started by Faustino Castillo, a Cuban immigrant, who came to Key West as a skilled Cigar roller to work in the burgeoning cigar industry. He opened his first store at Virginia and Packer Streets in 1926 and split his time between shifts at the cigar factory and running his store with his wife Ana Luisa. He quickly outgrew this location in a former house and move to 600 Fleming Street in the 1930s. He moved once again and settled at the present location in 1949.

Fausto's is a great family owned neighborhood grocery store and is renowned for carrying a great variety of gourmet and local products. You'll find an excellent selection of pasture-raised, antibiotic-free pork from the Neiman Ranch, Kobe beef, grass-fed beef, and organic chicken. Of course, you can also choose from a large variety of fresh seafood daily. Fausto's stocks an excellent variety of fresh fruits and vegetables including organic products. In addition, they also cook a delicious variety of food in their deli. You can check out their menu on their website to see what they have cooked up that day including soups, entrees, and sides. If you don't see what you're looking for they can prepare sandwiches, fried chicken, or any other needs for picnics, fishing and sailing day trips. They even deliver within a reasonable distance in the Lower Keys for a minimum order of 25 dollars.

You don't have go to the liquor store for wine and beer. Fausto's has a super selection of varietal wines as well as all of the popular domestic and imported beers as well as an increasing number of craft beer choices.

They have two locations to serve you with the original at 522 Fleming Street and another at 1105 White Street.

Fausto's on White Street. Photo by Mark Lee.

Popular Locals Activities

1. Beat the heat and enjoy a morning walk, run, or bike ride. There's lots of reasons to get up and enjoy the island as the sun comes up. It's the coolest and quietest time of the morning. I like to get out and get a cup of coffee at the marina and take a walk along the docks.

2. Head to the beach and watch the sunrise. It's a great time to enjoy the sun and water before the crowd hits the shore. Also one of the best times to take pictures. Some of my favorite pictures that I've taken in Key West were around sunrise and a little after. There's a special glow that comes with the first rays.

3. Get out on the water in a boat. Not only is it a great way to cool off, but there's a lot going on in the water. With all of the marine life that inhabits the Florida Keys, it's a lot of fun to snorkel the reefs and enjoy seeing the wildlife.

4. Go fishing. Even locals go out with guides sometimes and some of the best fishing to be done is down in the Florida Keys. If you have your own boat then take off and go on your own.

5. If you like lobster then head out and catch your own. There are two distinct lobster seasons, mini season, and regular season. The mini season last for two days on July 26-27, 2017 and then regular season runs from August 6 thru March 31, 2018. You need both a saltwater fishing license and lobster license to catch these spiny rascals. You'll also need to know the rules and bag limits so check the Florida Fish and Wildlife website to be in the know and compliant. The penalties can be pretty stiff if you're not. www.myfwc.com/fishing/saltwater/recreational/lobster

6. Take a picnic and hit the beach. Fort Zachary Taylor has great picnic facilities and a good beach also. Smathers is a nice long beach and runs along South Roosevelt. Higg's Beach has good volleyball facilities and a children's playground across the road from the beach in the park.

7. Learn to kite surf. It always looks like so much fun, but when I picture my 275 pound frame being tossed around like a rag doll and slammed on the beach I am jarred back to reality. I'll leave the kite surfing to the professionals like Paul Menta. He makes it look easy!

8. Take a sunset cruise. Those with a sailboat or powerboat take advantage of this when they can. If you don't have a boat catch ride with a friend.

9. Catch those local's discounts after the tourists leave. Usually in June, the locals appreciation starts with various businesses offering discounts to the locals with a local ID. Some of the restaurants run ads in the Key West Citizen advertising off season specials that you don't have to be a local to enjoy.

10. Enjoy the arts. One of the perks to being a local is you get to enjoy the traveling musicians that come through. At this time, a new amphitheater is being constructed to be venue for future performances. This exciting new development should be completed by September 2017.

You can also enjoy special programs and exhibits sponsored by the local museums. This past winter the Key West Art and Historical Society hosted an evening of Ernest Hemingway's favorite cocktails with author Phillip Greene and Hemingway's grandson, John Hemingway.

WHERE'S THE BEACH

First a few words about the beaches of Key West and the Florida Keys. The Florida Keys are basically a long chain of coral islands. In others words they are rocky and as such you're not going to find any of those wide sandy bottom beaches like you may be used to on the mainland. However, the beaches of Key West are really beautiful and have lots of nice coconut palms and soft sand that has been brought in to make them more user friendly. You'll be hard pressed to find a more beautiful beach to relax on. Also you will find that a lot of them have some great places to snorkel and see some of the cool fish and wildlife that inhabit these tropical waters. You'll find almost all of the beach action on the Atlantic side of the island. I have tried to give a good description of all of the major beaches in Key West and let you know what is available at each so check it out and enjoy!

SMATHERS BEACH

Smathers Beach is the largest beach on the island and parallels A1A also known as South Roosevelt Blvd. When you cross the Cow Key Channel Bridge and come onto Key West you will want to take a left at the light onto South Roosevelt Blvd and follow it to Smathers. This is definitely the longest beach and it runs for about two miles. You'll find plenty of nice soft sand on the beach and ample parking along the road side. Also, scattered along the parking area along the beach you will see food trucks. Smathers has restrooms, showers, volley ball areas, Jet Ski rentals, and a boat ramp.

HIGGS BEACH

Higgs Beach can be found just to the south of the White Street Pier. It offers a nice white sand, 16.5 acre beach area perfect for swimming and sunbathing. On the beach side there are some good volley ball facilities as well as beach service for chair and umbrella rentals. You can also rent kayaks and paddle boards from the beach service. Across the street in the park there is a nice children's playground as well as tennis and pickle ball courts. Salute on the Beach is a really good Italian Restaurant that is beachfront and offers a great menu as well as view to enjoy. There is ample parking for bicycles, cars, and scooters at Higgs.

FORT ZACHARY TAYLOR HISTORIC STATE PARK
This large state park which covers 54 acres it home to what many consider to be the best beach on the island. This facility is on the Southwest side of Key West where the Atlantic Ocean meets the Gulf of Mexico. It is also the location of what most consider to be the best beach on the island. The beach here is large and sandy and has good areas for swimming and snorkeling. You can rent chairs and umbrellas as well as rafts and snorkel equipment . There is fishing in designated areas along the rock jetty. If you want to bring a picnic there are excellent areas to set up with grills and picnic tables. The Cayo Hueso Café is also open from 10 a.m. – 6 p.m. and offers breakfast, lunch, and snack food with a dining area that overlooks the ocean.

SOUTH BEACH
South Beach is a cozy inlet beach tucked away between The Southernmost Resort and the southern end of Duval Street. This beach is popular with the locals and tourists. You can rent chairs and umbrellas here at this scenic retreat. It is said that Tennessee Williams, the famous author and playwright, enjoyed a daily swim here. You will not find a lot of parking in this area and its best accessed by scooter or bicycle. The Southernmost Beach Café is an open air restaurant also located here offering breakfast, lunch, dinner, and full bar.

REST BEACH
This is a beach front park found just to the north of the White Street Pier. It has picnic facilities and shoreline for wading and shelling. It is an excellent location for sunrise photos in the morning.

SIMONTON STREET BEACH

This is the smallest beach for people that I have found on the island. I stumbled upon it one morning when I was out for a scooter ride. It is at the north end of Simonton Street and has parking available for a few cars as well as bikes, and scooters. There is a concrete pier that goes out into the water and a small sandy beach for sunning. You'll also find a swimming area here. This is possibly the least crowded beach that I have seen. I've never seen more than four or five people here at any given time. It has a nice view out to the Gulf side of Key West and also Sunset Key, the pricy luxury retreat that is accessible by water only.

DOG BEACH

This is a small beach just for dogs as its name plainly states. It's rocky and slippery and best suited for a splash about for man's best friend. It is just to the right of Louis Backyard Restaurant at the end of Vernon Street.

South Beach at the Atlantic end of Duval Street. Photo by Mark Lee.

Key West

FESTIVAL
FAVORITES

FESTIVAL FAVORITES

If you look at a calendar of events for the Florida Keys, it's easy to see that something is going on down here year round. There is some kind of fun activity, event, or festival all of the time and why not, the weather is great and the islands are beautiful. Some events are built around food, drink, music, and even some about the famous people that have lived here at one time or another. More often than not you'll also find that many of the events benefit charities. Folks that live in Key West and The Florida Keys love to have a good time and raise money doing it for a worthy cause. I've been fortunate to enjoy a lot of different events down here and in this chapter, I'll tell you about some of the most popular events that are held in Key West. In another chapter I'll also give you a month by month breakdown of the many cool things that will be happening this year in Key West.

CONCH REPUBLIC CUP

Key West Cuba Race Week
www.conchrepubliccup.org

This historic race was started in 1997 by Peter Goldsmith and Michelle Geslin with the help of the Key West Sailing Club and Commodore Esrich of the Hemingway International Yacht Club of Cuba. It started as a direct race to Varadero, Cuba but has since added Havana as a second destination. The Key West to Cuba race is now a three leg event which is first from Key West to Varadero, then Varadero to Havana and back to Key West from Havana. While in Cuba, there is built in downtime to explore its cultural offerings and build relationships with its hosts.

Although this event encourages cultural exchange and goodwill I guess you could say that our governments have not always shared this attitude. Due to this the race was on a 13 year hiatus due to intervention of the US government. When the sailors returned from Cuba after the 2003 race, their boats were stopped and boarded and the government seized some of their cameras and equipment. Also, principals of the Key West Club were accused, but never convicted of "trading with the enemy. Now that relations with our two countries have improved and many of the restrictions have been dropped, the race can be held with without fear of government reprisal.

The mission of the Conch Republic Cup states, "The goal of the founders and members of CRC has always been to support the Cuban and American people in their return to sailing and racing between the Southernmost Point in the US and Cuba." This popular event is a cultural exchange through sport. It attracts sailors from all over the United States with more than 200 sailors participating in this year's event hailing from 13 states. For more information check out their website and come experience it for yourself.

KEY WEST FOOD & WINE FESTIVAL

www.keywestfoodandwinefestival.com

The Key West Wine and Food Festival is a five day event held every January that attracts attendees from around the world who are drawn to this tropical island nation for a week of food, wine, and fun. It is a series of wine and food themed events that show off the wide array of wines and original cuisine that Key West has to offer in some of the islands iconic locales. I can't think of a better place to be in January than Key West and The Florida Keys. While the rest of the country is shivering in a deep freeze, I get to enjoy some of the best cuisine around while dressed in shorts and a casual shirt in the tropical sunshine. Some of the highlights of the week include the "Henry Flagler's Welcome Party, and Key West "Uncorked." The "Welcome Party" takes place beachside at the historic Casa Marina Hotel. The Casa Marina was built in the early 1900s as a destination for the passengers that traveled to Key West on the Overseas Railway that was built by millionaire visionary Henry Flagler. During this event you have a chance to sip some delicious wines and sample bites of exquisite cuisine expertly prepared by Executive Chef Alex Beaumont. Key West "Uncorked" is a fun filled event held in Old Town Key West. Participants get the chance to enjoy tasting wines in over 25 locations as they check out the funky shops, boutiques, and galleries of the area.

Some other favorites include neighborhood strolls through some of Old Town's iconic sections as well as a Sunset Tasting at the new Margaritaville Resort on the waterfront. Tickets for the 2018 event are on sale now. See their website for more details.

COW KEY CHANNEL BRIDGE RUN

COW KEY CHANNEL RUN

www.cowkeybridgerun.com

Finally I've found an athletic event where I can excel. It's the kind of event that can appeal to the non-athlete and underachiever in all of us. It's also the kind of race where you don't have to get up early and you don't have far to run. In fact this race starts at 12 noon and the record finish so far is a blazing 23.1 seconds. This is the Cow Key Channel Bridge Run, the world's only zero K run, which is held every April and runs from one side of the Cow Key Channel Bridge to the other. Have no fear because this sucker isn't the Seven Mile Bridge. If you can walk, jog or run 300 feet then you too can participate in this wacky, fun event and get a t-shirt.

It got its start as a joke after the athlete in a group of friends had talked some of his other friends into running a 5k with them. After a late night of drinking you can imagine that the results were less than impressive and maybe a little punitive for the participants. A few weeks later the same friend tried to get them to enter the Seven Mile Bridge Run and one of them said the only bridge he would ever run would be the Cow Key Channel Bridge. And the rest as they say is history and this Zero K event was born. David Sloan, co-producer of the event, said that it started as "A way to score a trophy and a t-shirt without breaking a sweat."

Of course, all of this is done in fun and jest and there are many ways to win a prize. There are five different heats with the first being for those looking to set records in the "1st Place Contenders" and the fifth and final heat being for the "Last Place Contenders" who are the slowest to finish while maintaining forward motion. All of the participants get a cool t-shirt, designed new every year, and a chance to win one of the coveted Golden Calf Awards. The race starts at 12:00 p.m. sharp and the awards ceremony kicks off on the other side at 12:01 p.m. complete with live music, food trucks, full bar. If this sounds like your kind of event you can register online and then show up and show out. The participants start showing up on the Key West side around 10 am in their best attire or not. There are no dress codes or requirements, but there are lots of different awards based on costume. Just come looking for a good time and a lot of fun and you won't be disappointed.

KEY WEST SONGWRITERS FESTIVAL

www.keywestsongwritersfestival.com

What started off as a gathering of a few of Nashville's songwriters and local performers putting on a half dozen shows around town in 1995 has now grown into a full-fledged major attraction. The Key West Songwriters Festival is a chance to see over 50 shows put on by over 200 performers during a five day period every May. It is the largest gathering of its kind and attracts music lovers from around the US and worldwide to experience country music in The Conch Republic. You may not recognize the names, but you will definitely know some of their songs and appreciate their tunes. For the most part songwriters labor in anonymity while it is the star that sings the song on the radio or TV that you remember. This unique event gives the songwriter some time out of Nashville to shine on their own for a week as they perform in many of Key West's most popular bars and resorts. For the most part this event is free to attend and is a great chance to see a lot of quality performers in one place. You do see some of the up and coming stars of Nashville performing as well as some of the top song-writers. This year's free street concert on Saturday featured Maren Morris, Old Dominion, and Cam. The three hour show was held on the Main Stage on a blocked off Duval Street just past Sloppy Joe's Bar and drew a shoulder to shoulder crowd as they were wowed by some super entertainment. This is a great event and good chance to hear some cool music and have a vacation too.

THE KEY LIME FESTIVAL

www.keylimefestival.com

I can't think of anything that is more representative of Key West and the Florida Keys than the tiny citrus fruit knows as the Key Lime. After all Key West is the birthplace of the Key Lime Pie and you'll find shops all over town making anything from cookies to bbq sauce with this tangy citrus fruit. Therefore, it's just natural that David Sloan and a few of his friends would get together and turn this unique fruit into a one of a kind 4th of July weekend party. You'll find all kinds of fun filled events such as the Sip and Stroll. In this event fifteen of Key West's top bars compete for the Key Lime Cup by making the best Key Lime Martini and Margarita. The best part is that you get to participate in the judging and sample the drinks at six different stations that have been setup with the entries. There is also a Key Lime Pie Hop where you get to sample five of the island's best dessert offerings by checking in at the five different locations around Old Town Key West. You even get a souvenir T-shirt for the event when you register.

Of course, what kind of party would it be without a pie eating contest? Watch the hungry competitors as they try to devour an entire Key Lime Pie in less than 62 seconds, which is the current record set in 2016. The contest is free to watch and will be held around 11 a.m. on July 4th at the Ocean Key Resort on the Key West waterfront. Go to their website at www.keylimefestival.com to see a complete list of all the events and get registered for the wacky fun filled festival.

MEL FISHER DAYS

www.melfisherdays.melfisher.com

Mel Fisher was part dreamer, part visionary, and full time optimist. How else could you explain how a former chicken farmer from California would one day move to Key West and find a 450 million dollar fortune in treasure? Every day Mel would exclaim, "Today's the Day," as he set out in search of the Nuestra Senora de Atocha. The Atocha was a Spanish treasure ship overloaded with New World riches that sank in a hurricane in the waters off Key West in 1622. It was on its way back to Spain to deliver a cargo of gold, silver, and jewels.

Mel Fisher Days celebrates the anniversary of finding the Atocha and the discovery of its "Mother Load" of treasure on July 20, 1985. During this three day event you will have the opportunity to take a VIP tour of the Fisher Family's private Conservation Laboratory in their Maritime Museum. Learn what meticulous measures are taken by these scientists to carefully catalogue and preserve the artifacts that are retrieved from the ocean floor. There is also a dock party at the Schooner Wharf Bar on Saturday to further honor and celebrate Mel Fisher at one of his favorite former haunts. One of the salvage vessels that is used to hunt treasure, the JB Magruder, will be on display and available for tours. There will also be members from the Golden Crew of the Atocha Discovery on hand for you to meet and get autographs. There will be chances to win money and treasure prizes along with silent and live auction items available for bid.

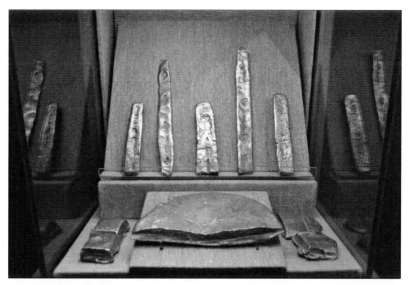

Picured here is some of the gold that Mel Fisher's crews have salvaged from the ocean floor. Photo by Mark Lee.

An exhibit with pictures of Hemingway's fishing yacht, Pilar, can be seen at his former home on Whitehead Street. Photo by Mark Lee.

Elaborate model of Hemingway's Pilar handmade and donated to charity by David Hemingway, Papa 2016. Photo credit David Hemingway

HEMINGWAY DAYS

www.fla-keys.com/hemingway-days

Ernest Hemingway landed in Key West with his wife Pauline in 1928 and this island nation has never been the same since. Prior to his arrival it was known as quiet little community made up of tough as shark skin native residents known as Conchs, as well as a mixture of Bahamian and Cuban expats. Little did they know that they were about to shed their former wrecker and rum running persona and become a haven for artists including writers, painters, and the like. Once Papa arrived and fell in love with its unmatched salt water fishing, breath taking scenery, and siren like watering holes it would be forever known as the home of Ernest Hemingway. His impressive home on Whitehead Street has a steady stream of daily visitors all looking for their piece of the Hemingway experience. There's also the two bars both proclaiming to be the place where Hemingway drank and both are correct. Although Captain Tony's may have been the original location of Sloppy Joe Russell's bar at 428 Greene Street, it is the Duval Street Sloppy Joes where the visage of Papa can be seen adoring the walls, T-shirts, key chains, and cups and is popularly accepted as the mecca where patrons wander in seeking their personal Hemingway experience and want to follow in Papas thirsty footsteps.

It was also here at Sloppy Joes in 1981 that the Hemingway Days Festival was spawned and its first Ernest Hemingway look alike, Tom Feeney, was named. Over the years it has continued to grow in popularity and has become one of the island's premier events of the year. It is held every year during the third week of July celebrating the birthday of its namesake which is July 21 and his accomplishments as an author and sportsman.

The weeklong festival features events such as the Marlin fishing tournament, Papa's birthday party, the running of the bulls, and the wildly popular Ernest Hemingway Look Alike Contests with its own series of events. I had occasion to speak with this year's winner, David Hemingway and got a Papa's eye view of just what it means to be a Papa and a part of this great celebration of one of Key West's most beloved former citizens.

Although he has the last name Hemingway, David stated that there was no relation. He will serve as this year's Papa throughout 2016-2017 until next year's contest and as such will always be invited back to judge the event for the rest of his life. His first trip to Key West was in the Coast Guard in the 1970s and he has returned as a tourist many times since then. He said that he has come down to the Keys with friends regularly throughout the years. They rent a home in Key Largo and Marathon and make it into Key West a couple of times during their stay. When questioned about his experience with the Look Alike Contest, Hemingway stated that his first time entering was back in 2010 and he won this year which was his seventh attempt. The contest starts on Wednesday at Sloppy Joes where all of the current year's contestants are introduced as well as the previous Papas in attendance. On Thursday, the recipients of the scholarships are announced which is a major part of the Hemingway Look Alike Society. Every year during the Festival, they raise money which goes to benefit deserving students attending the Florida Keys Community College. Much of this money for scholarships comes from an auction of donated items which is held during the judging of the Look Alike events. Many one of a kind items are put up for sale such as Craft Key West Rum made by Chef Paul Menta at his Key West Legal Rum Distillery. He has also donated a rum barrel autographed by all Papas in attendance which is always popular and brings top dollar.

David Hemingway shares a trait that was very characteristic of the late Ernest Hemingway in the fact that he greatly admires the Pilar. The Pilar was Ernest's much beloved fishing yacht which was built in the Wheeler Shipyard in Brooklyn, New York in 1934 for the sum of

$ 7495. It was named after both the heroine in his novel "For Whom the Bell Tolls,' as well as the nickname for his wife at the time, Pauline. Ernest spent many happy hours in the waters around Key West and Cuba chasing big game fish on his boat. David enjoys building replicas of the Pilar and has donated several of them to the auction to help raise scholarship funds. Just this year, he donated a beautiful half hull model mounted on a framed map of The Florida Keys and Cuba. He has also donated both a model of the Pilar in a bottle of Pilar

Rum as well as a hand painted large scale model of the elaborate fishing yacht. Other items such as art, food, wine, and dinners are given up for auction to raise money for these very deserving Florida Keys college students.

The first night of the actual Hemingway Look Alike contest is Thursday night with another preliminary round being held on Friday night as well. Saturday brings the running of the bulls which is kind of like the event in Pamplona, Spain but with one major exception, the bulls are not actually animals. Here in Key West the bulls are actually replicas on wheels. The streets are blocked off around Sloppy Joes for this fun filled event. The weeklong festival culminates on Saturday night with the naming of the winner of the Ernest Hemingway Look Alike contest for this year.

David Hemingway said that the Papas are very popular around the island and revered for their position and treated as celebrities. He said that this year he had a film crew following him around wherever he went. Everywhere the Papas go people want their autograph and a picture taken with them. The Papas do like to kick back a bit when the contest is not on and some of them enjoy going to the Bull and Whistle, a bar at the corner of Duval and Caroline Streets, where they can enjoy the open air atmosphere and a cool drink. They may also go to the Two Friends Patio Restaurant which features karaoke and is a favorite of some of the Papas in the evening.

When asked what his favorite part of Hemingway Days is, David said without hesitation, "The friendship, and fellowship with his fellow participants and Papas, it's like a fraternity." When talking about his experiences, he told me about his good friend, Michael Groover, that he had met during the contest who hails from Savannah, Georgia. He is a docking pilot on the Savannah River who guides massive container ships to the docks at the Georgia Ports Authority facility in the Savannah. He said that he has been a guest of the Captain and his wife at their home and has also been hosted with others Papas by the couple at a gathering in the coastal Georgia city that they organized. Part of Hemingway's duties will be to come together with others Papas at what is called the mid-year gathering in the spring of 2017. They gather in various places in the Southeastern US and include wives and girlfriends.

This all sounds like a great time and something that I would like to do, but there's one catch for me. I don't quite resemble Ernest Hemingway yet, but I'm working on it. Give me a few years to grow out my grey beard and get a little more "salt" in my hair and count me in. I can't wait.

David Hemingway was the winner of the 2016 Ernest Hemingway look-alike contest. Photo by Jean Cole.

FANTASY FEST

Let's just call this Halloween on steroids for adults and if you're packing a bag for this event you probably won't exceed the airlines weight limit. Costumes for Fantasy Fest in many cases are painted on and clothes are sometimes an afterthought during this yearly ten daylong celebration.

Fantasy Fest started back in the 1978 when two Key West locals recognized the need to stir things up to increase business in town. Back in those days things pretty much shut down and workers were laid off during the off season. They said that a party or festival was just what was needed to bring people to town to enjoy what is really one of the nicest seasons of the year. The first Fantasy Fest was held the next year in 1979.

The first event of this ten day party is family friendly and is known as the Goombay Festival. This is a street party held in the Bahama Village neighborhood that includes arts and crafts, food, and music. On the same evening over at the Casa Marina Hotel they'll hold a coronation for the King and Queen who'll reign over Fantasy Fest for its duration.

During Fantasy Fest there are balls, costume contests, fundraisers, and plenty of revelry. In many ways, this ten day Bacchanalia has grown into something that rivals Mardi Gras in New Orleans. There are neighborhood parades as well as the main parade which proceeds from one end of Duval Street to the other. This parade features elaborately adorned floats with a competition for the best decorated.

This bears repeating so listen closely: Fantasy Fest is a ten day celebration for adults. There is a lot of alcohol, mirth, and merriment enjoyed in an atmosphere with inhibitions thrown to wind. If you go, just keep in mind that this is not Halloween for the kiddies, best to leave them at home. Now having said that, pack your costumes and go have a ball!

Parrot Heads look on as Toby Keith and Mac McAnally entertain at the 2016 Meeting of the Minds. Photo credit Mark Lee.

MEETING OF THE MINDS

www.phip.com

Although most of this event is for members only, it's hard to leave out my favorite event of the year. My wife and I really enjoy our early November get away to Key West and have met some of the nicest people in the process.

Meeting of the Minds is the yearly gathering of Parrot Heads from around the country who come to Key West and take over the Casa Marina Resort for the week. During this weeklong celebration of Buffetmania we get to enjoy a daily diet of some great Trop Rock music on a stage that is set up beachside at the hotel. There are also two crystal clear pools in the area as well as food and drinks poolside. Sounds like a literal paradise, what else would you need?

The first year that we went, Jimmy Buffet and the Coral Reefers performed on Thursday night with other members of his band like, Peter Mayer and his son Brendan performing at other times throughout the weekend. The event's organizer, Andrew Talbert, does a super job in lining up some of the most talented musicians from around the country. Besides all of the music on site there is also a Street Festival on Friday with part of Duval Street blocked and a band playing on the stage in the middle of the street near Margaritaville most of the afternoon.

In addition to the music there is a minimart set up with vendors inside the hotel with anything from books and photos to tropical clothing. On one side of the room the DJ's from Radio Margaritaville broadcast live all week. Not just here to party all week, the clubs also raise a lot of money for charity through blood drives, fun walks, and raffles. If all of this sounds too good to be true, then come and check it out for yourself. First you'll need to be a member in good standing of a Parrot Head Club and then next you'll need to register to attend the Meeting of the Minds.

This event is wildly popular and has to limit attendance so if you want to go you'll need to act early. Go to their website and check things out and maybe we'll see you there!

Jimmy Bufffet and Mac McAnnally performed with the rest of the Coral Reefer Band at the 2015 MOTM. Photo by Mark Lee.

37TH ANNUAL KEY WEST WORLD CHAMPIONSHIP POWERBOAT RACES

www.superboat.com/race-schedule/key-west-schedule

This event is kind of like a NASCAR race however, it's held on the water. Just imagine standing on the Truman waterfront and hearing the thunderous roar down the way. As the boats approach, you can see the spray and feel the roar as they get closer and finally pass right in front of you churning up the lime green waters behind them. This year will be the 37th annual Powerboat Championship Race and I consider it to be one of my favorite events.

I've been to Sprint Cup races and this has a lot of the same excitement with one thing that makes it even better, it's in Key West. On Sunday night before Race Week they have a boat parade down Duval Street and you get a chance to preview all of the contenders. The actual racing starts on Wednesday with others held throughout the day on Friday. On Friday night Duval Street is blocked off for the big street party and another chance to see the boats and their crews up close and personal. On the off days there is time for working on boats and test runs out on the course.

The final and championship race is held on Sunday with the World Champion being named. The powerboat races are a lot of fun and with the rest of the country starting to feel the coming of winter this time of year, it's a great time to enjoy the sun and some nice weather in south Florida.

Powerboats race by on the Truman waterfront during Powerboat week. Photo by Mark Lee. Permission of Superboat International.

Key West

WHAT'S HAPPENING

JANUARY

Jan. 12, 2017 – Jan. 15, 2017
35th Annual Key West Literary Seminar
www.kwls.org

Literary aficionados from around the world are to gather for readings, discussions, and lectures led by some of contemporary literature's most acclaimed writers. Presenters include celebrated biographer Robert Caro, Pulitzer Prize winner Annette Gordon-Reid, and noted journalists/authors Gail Collins and Joe Klein. A first-come, first-seated Sunday afternoon session is free and open to the public.

Jan. 13, 2017 – Jan. 14, 2017 Location: Key West
57th Annual Key West House & Garden Tours

Tour a series of elegant and unique private homes of Key West, ranging from exquisite restorations to creative renovations, and the interior design that complements each. March tours are offered 10 a.m. to 4 p.m. each day. Transportation between homes is optional, via Conch Train. Tickets are $30. Proceeds help benefit the Old Island Restoration Foundation.

Jan. 14, 2017 – Jan. 15, 2017 Location: Key West
Category: Arts & Culture
12th Annual Florida Keys Seafood Festival
www.fkcfa.org/seafood-festival1

A family-friendly event with local fresh Keys' seafood, drinks, marine-related crafts, youth activities, and live music. $5 admission per person; hours open from 11 a.m. – 8 p.m. on Saturday; 11 a.m. to 5 p.m. on Sunday, at Bayview Park, Truman Avenue and Jose Marti Drive.

Jan. 15, 2017
Key West Half Marathon & 5k Run
www.keywesthalfmarathon.com/

Recognized by Runner's World magazine as one of the ten great half-marathons of the winter season, the race follows a 13.1-mile course that includes Old Town Key West and the scenic waterfront. Now in its 19th year, the race typically attracts American and international runners to compete in Key West's balmy January climate. Named as one of the United States' leading winter half marathons in Runner's World, February, 2014; the same magazine included in its list of Best Destination Half Marathons; in April, 2015; Bucket List Best Half Marathons, and most recently in December, 2015 was ranked among 13 must-do U.S. half-marathons by Competitor.com.

Jan. 15, 2017 – Jan. 20, 2017 Location: Key West
30th Annual Quantum Key West Race Week 2017
www.keywestraceweek.com

The annual race week challenge features world-class competition and yachting teams from more than 12 countries and 24 American states. More than 100 racing yachts typically compete for class championships in this international regatta. To view the action, fans can book seats on spectator boats ranging from excursion catamarans to historic tall ships or from land at Key West's Atlantic-front restaurants, resorts, and beaches.

Jan. 21, 2017 – Jan. 22, 2017 Location: Key West
Category: Fishing
Key West Kingfish Mayhem
www.keywestkingfishmayhem.com

Big fish, big money! Come fish for some of the largest kingfish in Florida Keys waters in this new tournament. Fishing headquartered at Stock Island Marina. First prize could earn $15,000 cash, based on a 50-boat field.

Jan. 25, 2017 – Jan. 29, 2017 Location: Key West Category:
Arts & Culture
Key West Food & Wine Festival
www.keywestfoodandwinefestival.com

Top chefs and restaurateurs display culinary creativity and the Keys' indigenous cuisine in a flavorful schedule of events for food lovers.

Highlights include the lively "Old Town Uncorked," neighborhood wine strolls, food and wine pairings, intriguing seminars, winemaker dinner series, and a grand tasting.

Jan. 28, 2017 – Jan. 29, 2017 Location: Key West Category: Arts & Culture

32nd Annual Key West Craft Show

keywestartcenter.com/craft.html

Tens of thousands of attendees browse and buy among juried artisans and crafters who gather to display their talents at this popular outdoor festival on lower Whitehead Street in historic Old Town Key West.

Jan. 29, 2017 Location: Key West

23rd Annual Key West Master Chefs Classic

www.marchouse.org/masterchefsclassic

Local restaurants vie for top honors in appetizer, entrée, and dessert categories. Attendees sample the culinary treats while judges pick the winners. The show is held from 4-7 p.m. at the Westin Key West Resort & Marina pier. Event proceeds benefit the nonprofit Monroe Association for ReMARCable Citizens.

Jan. 22, 2017 – Feb. 3, 2017 Location: Key West Category: Arts & Culture

Conch Republic Cup, Key West Cuba Race Week

www.conchrepubliccup.org

The CRC is a historic race that started in 1997 with direct race to Varadero then expanded to Havana in 1999. The triangle race as it has been coined is a traditional race to Cuba that allows the racer to complete a triangle between KW and two Cuban cities – Varadero and Havana. The CRC is a non-profit organization with the mission to introduce as many of the US sailing community to Cuba as possible as well as revitalize racing in Cuba

FEBRUARY

Feb. 14, 2017 Location: Key West
34th Annual Wesley House Valentine's Day Gala
This signature fundraiser features some of Key West's most talented performing artists, the island's largest silent auction, open bar, dancing, and an elegant and abundant dinner buffet. The Theme this year is Hat's Off to Edith (Amsterdam) and Good Knight Edward. Located at Curry Mansion Inn, 511 Caroline Street 6:30-9:30 p.m. VIP tickets also available. Purchase tickets online.

Feb. 25, 2017 – Feb. 26, 2017 Location: Key West
Key West Garden Club Gardens Tour
www.keywestgardenclub.com/Open_to_All.html
From 10 a.m. to 3 p.m. both days, peek behind the walls and visit beautiful private gardens. Admission is $20 per person. Located at West Martello Tower on Higgs Beach.

Feb. 25, 2017 – Feb. 26, 2017
Location: Key West Category: Arts & Culture
Old Island Days Art Festival
www.keywestartcenter.com/festival.html
The 52nd annual juried outdoor fine art festival features oil paintings, watercolors, sculpture, photography, and other offerings by more than 100 artists from around the United States and beyond. The event takes place on lower Whitehead Street in historic Old Town.

Feb. 28, 2017 – Mar. 27, 2017
Happy Birthday Tennessee Williams!
www.twkw.org/events.html
Celebrate the 106th birthday of Tennessee Williams and his life in Key West during the month of March. Highlights include a series of classic movies adapted from Williams' award winning plays, a poetry contest, artist challenge, staged readings from his plays, letters & journals, a film forum, and much more. Visitors are invited to tour the educational and historic Tennessee Williams Key West Exhibit, at 513

MARCH

55th Annual Conch Shell Blowing Contest
www.oirf.org

An island tradition for over 50 years, this unique contest celebrates the historic importance of conch in the Keys and features contestants in several age categories attempting to make "music" with fluted conch shells. Contest located in the garden of the Oldest House, 322 Duval Street, free and open to all ages. Registration begins at 10 a.m., contest starts at noon.

Mar. 13, 2017 – Mar. 16, 2017 Location: Key West
Category: Fishing
March Merkin Invitational Permit Tournament
www.marchmerkin.com

A charity flats-and-fly-only tournament with a twist – in addition to catch and release, anglers earn extra points for tagging their caught fish. Held at the Key West Yacht Harbor Marina on Stock Island.

Mar. 17, 2017 – Mar. 18, 2017 Location: Key West
57th Annual Key West House & Garden Tours
www.oirf.org/page.php?p=tours

Tour a series of elegant and unique private homes of Key West, ranging from exquisite restorations to creative renovations, and the interior design that complements each. March tours are offered 10 a.m. to 4 p.m. each day. Transportation between homes NOT included. Tickets are $30. Proceeds help benefit the Old Island Restoration Foundation.

APRIL

Apr. 2, 2017 Location: Key West

Fourth Annual Cow Key Channel Bridge Run

www.cowkeybridgerun.com

Feel like running across a bridge in the Florida Keys without waking up early or breaking a sweat? Join zany-dressed participants for the world's only Zero K across one of the shortest bridges in the Keys. The event is free to watch.

Apr. 7, 2017 – Apr. 9, 2017 Location: Key West
Category: Fishing

Key West Fishing Tournament Kickoff

www.keywestfishingtournament.com

Traditionally, 15 target species and $5,000 in cash prizes await anglers. Participants vie for cash awards for catching the heaviest dolphin, kingfish, cobia, black fin tuna, mackerel, mutton snapper, wahoo, mangrove snapper, and grunt. In addition, cash awaits boat teams that score the most releases of tarpon, permit, bonefish, barracuda, marlin, and sailfish. Awards also are presented each year in the junior division for anglers under age 15.

Apr. 21, 2017 – Apr. 30, 2017 Location: Key West
Category: Arts & Culture

35th Annual Conch Republic Independence Celebration

www.conchrepublic.com/home

With activities ranging from wacky bed race to a lighthearted sea battle featuring tall ships, the Conch Republic's 10-day birthday party showcases the independent and eccentric spirit that characterizes the Florida Keys.

168

Apr. 25, 2017 – Apr. 30, 2017 Location: Key West
Category: Fishing
The Final Sail
www.bluewatermovements.com/final_sail
This four-day challenge is the 'grand finale' of the 4-leg Quest for the
Crest Sailfish Series. Team cash prizes include up to $50,000 for first
place and $18,000 and $10,000 to second- and third-place anglers, plus
trophies, respectively. Early entry fee is available.

Apr. 27, 2017 – Apr. 30, 2017 Location: Key West
Key West Paddle Classic
Sue Cooper 305-304-4259
www.paddleguru.com/races/KeyWestPaddleClassic2016
Presented by Lazy Dog Adventures, the challenge includes a 12-mile
Elite Race around the island and a 4-mile open race. Other events in-
clude a kick-off registration party, paddleboard clinics and races for
kids.

MAY

May 5 – 7, 2017 Location Key West
Papio Kinetic Sculpture Parade
www.papioskineticparade.com

If one man's junk is another man's treasure, then the late Key Largo folk artist Stanley Papio was a treasure hunter extraordinaire. Fans of "outsider art" can celebrate the renegade metal sculptor's legacy with a people-powered parade of mobile sculptures crafted in the spirit of his extraordinary creations. The Papio Kinetic Sculpture Parade features colorful sculptural floats, tricycles with exotically costumed riders, fantastically decorated bicycles and other moving works of art — all powered by human effort alone — and are to follow a route along the length of Key West's Duval Street.

May. 10, 2017 – May. 14, 2017 Location: Key West
Category: Arts & Culture
Key West Songwriters' Festival
www.keywestsongwritersfestival.com

The 22nd annual showcase of musical magic features America's foremost performing songwriters, with concerts staged in intimate, audience-friendly island settings.

JUNE

June 10, 2017
Fifth Annual VFW Fishing Tournament
www.vfwpost3911.org/fishing-tournament

Sponsored by the Southernmost VFW Post 3911, this family oriented tournament offers cash prizes for dolphin, wahoo, tuna, snapper, and grouper, along with prizes for heaviest fish by a lady angler, heaviest fish by a juvenile angler, pee-wee, and active service member. Heaviest Dolphin is worth $2,500. Entry fee $200 per boat By May 19, 2017; $250 per boat after May 19, 2017. All proceeds benefit disabled and veterans in need throughout Monroe County.

Contact: Curly McGinn (305) 304-1182
Email: curlybluemarlin@gmail.com

Jun. 10, 2017 Location: Key West
Key West Island Swim: FKCC Swim Around Key West
www.fkccswimaroundkeywest.com

The officially sanctioned event is a 12.5-mile swim clockwise around the island of Key West that is open to all age groups. Individual swimmers and relay teams can compete. The route takes swimmers through the waters of the Atlantic Ocean and Gulf of Mexico, ending where they began at Higgs Beach.

JULY

Jul. 1, 2017 – Jul. 4, 2017 Location: Key West
Category: Arts & Culture
Fifth Annual Key Lime Festival
www.keylimefestival.com

A wacky talent show, pie-eating and cooking contests and other tasty temptations await Key West visitors during the fourth annual Key Lime Festival. A Key Lime martini Sip and Stroll, Key lime rum sampling and distillery tour as well as a new Key Lime Pie Hop are among events to kick off the four-day tasty fest.

Jul. 8, 2017 – Jul. 11, 2017 Location: Key West
Category: Fishing
Del Brown Permit Tournament
www.delbrownpermit.weebly.com

Anglers fly-fish on the flats in a challenge that honors the late angling pioneer Del Brown, who caught and released more than 500 permit off the Keys. Professionals and guides are allowed to compete as well.

Jul. 18, 2017 – Jul. 23, 2017 Location: Key West
Category: Arts & Culture
Hemingway Days
www.sloppyjoes.com/look-alike-contest/lal-schedule

The 37th annual celebration of the legendary author's work and lifestyle features literary readings, the Running of the Bulls, a short story competition, fishing tournament, 5k Run and Paddleboard Race, Sloppy Joe's Look-Alike Contest, and a birthday "party" commemorating Ernest's July 21st birthday.

Jul. 19, 2017 – Jul. 22, 2017 Location: Key West
Category: Fishing
Bacardi Oakheart Key West Marlin Tournament
www.keywestmarlin.com

Anglers ply the waters once fished by novelist Ernest Hemingway, vying for $50,000 in guaranteed cash prizes. Held in conjunction with Key West's annual Hemingway Days festival, the event awards $25,000 to the first-place team. Teams can enter one fun fish (dolphin, tuna, wahoo or released sailfish) per day to add to their point total.

Jul. 22, 2017 Location: Key West
Category: Arts & Culture
Hemingway 5K Sunset Run & Paddleboard Race
www.keywesthalfmarathon.com/hemingway-5k-sunset-run-paddle-board-race

This is the original and oldest ongoing 5K Run in Key West and takes place as part of the the annual Hemingway Days Festival. The race course is a scenic flat course that runs past Key West's most famous landmarks including the Ernest Hemingway Home, the iconic Southernmost Point, and the famous Green Parrot Bar. Visit website for more details.

AUGUST

Aug. 31, 2017 – Sep. 4, 2017 Location: Key West
Category: Arts & Culture

Eighth Annual Key West Brewfest
800-354-4455
www.keywestbrewfest.com

More than 150 beers and micro-brews are on tap at this "tasty" annual event that benefits the charitable efforts of the Key West Sunrise Rotary Club of the Conch Republic. Events from beer dinners, beer brunches, happy hour parties, pool parties, late-night parties, seminars, and the Signature Tasting Festival Event are some of the offered activities.

SEPTEMBER

Sep. 8, 2017 – Sep. 10, 2017 Location: Key West
Category: Fishing
Robert James Sales S.L.A.M. Celebrity Tournament
305-664-2002

In the first of three tournaments in the annual Redbone Celebrity Tournament Series, also called The Trilogy, anglers target tarpon, permit, and bonefish to achieve the coveted "flats grand slam." The event raises funds for the fight against cystic fibrosis.

Sep. 15, 2017 – Oct. 15, 2017 Location: Key West
Category: Arts & Culture
Wine Dine Key West
www.winedinekeywest.com

Dine, Shop, and Relax during this month-long moveable feast. Cuisine connoisseurs can enjoy multi-course prix fixe meals at several Key West restaurants during Wine Dine Key West. Restaurants include casual waterfront spots, trendy bistros, eateries specializing in fresh Florida Keys seafood, and award-winning gourmet emporiums. Local spas and chic boutiques are also participating in the celebration. Register free online.

OCTOBER

Oct. 6, 2017 – Oct. 8, 2017 Location: Key West
SoMo Marathon & Half Marathon
lizlovekw@gmail.com
www.somomarathon.com

This event is one of a kind! Imagine running through the southern-most island in the United States while enjoying a break from the ordinary. The Southernmost Marathon & Half promises just that- 26.2 or 13.1 miles of ocean and gulf views, as well as iconic Key West land-marks. A full weekend of events include the race and a Sunday Paddle Board race for the Special Olympics of Monroe County.

Oct. 13, 2017 – Oct. 16, 2017 Location: Key West
Category: Arts & Culture
Sixth Annual Standup Paddle Invitational 2017
305-923-0288
www.paddleguru.com/races/SUPInvitational2017KeyWest

Join a 2-mile paddle board and beach obstacle course to support Spe-cial Olympics Florida Monroe County. This all-levels event is fun for beginners and experienced paddlers alike. Race is to be a loop style course offering a great view for our spectators. Registration fee $35. Board rentals available through Lazy Dog.

Oct. 20, 2017 – Oct. 29, 2017 Location: Key West
Category: Arts & Culture
38th Annual Key West Fantasy Fest
305-296-1817
www.fantasyfest.com

This outrageous 10-day costuming and masking celebration features flamboyant masquerade competitions including one for pets, a head-dress ball, exuberant promenades, street fairs, and a grand parade that stars marching groups, island-style bands and lavish floats. The 2017 festival theme is "Time Travel Unravels."

Oct. 27, 2017 Location: Key West
The Smallest Parade In The Universe
www.thesmallestparadeintheuniverse.com

A dazzling event from 5-9 p.m., at the corner of Caroline and William streets, at Key West Waterfront Brewery. Artists, craftsmen, model makers, and creative types are encouraged to participate, making floats no larger than 18 inches! Proceeds benefit the MARC house. Up to $2,000 in prizes.

NOVEMBER

Nov. 5, 2017 – Nov. 12, 2017 Location: Key West
37th Annual Key West World Championship Races
305-296-6166
www.superboat.com/race-schedule/key-west-schedule

Super Boat International returns with teams from all around the world who compete April through October in the National Series Points races and conclude in November for the famous Key West World Championships. High-speed offshore powerboats race in Key West Harbor and surrounding waters to continue Key West's longstanding tradition in this annual challenge, known internationally as the Indianapolis 500 of powerboat racing. A portion of the 6.5-mile course runs through Key West Harbor, meaning smooth water where racers can achieve speeds above 140 mph and provide fans breathtaking displays of skill and power.

Nov. 15 – 19, 2017, Location: Key West
Key West Film Festival
Beth Moyes 305-747-8563
www.kwfilmfest.com

Showcasing films that exhibit excellence in storytelling, the festival's lineup is to feature screenings and special events hosted at landmark venues throughout Key West, including the San Carlos Institute, Studios of Key West, and Key West Theater. The four-day program is to include several films from multiple genres and categories as well as social events with filmmakers, actors and film lovers.

DECEMBER

Dec. 1, 2017 – Dec. 31, 2017 Location: Key West
Category: Arts & Culture
Key West Holiday Fest
www.keywestchristmas.org

Each year a wide range of seasonal celebrations takes place throughout Key West during the month of December. Events include the lighting of the Harbor Walk of Lights, tours of historic decorated inns, a holiday parade, and much more.

Dec. 9, 2017 Location: Key West
Key West Triathlon and Expo
us.eventbu.com/fort-lauderdale/2017-tri-key-west-sprint-and-olympic-triathlon-and-duathlon/239635

The Key West Triathlon and Expo expects to host a maximum of 1,000 participants and some of the sport's best known triathletes; TRIKW allows you to bask in the warm weather and the waters of the Atlantic Ocean while the rest of the country is experiencing winter. Olympic and Sprint distances.

Dec. 8, 2017 – Dec. 10, 2017 Location: Key West
Inaugural Key West Grand Prix of the Sea
(407) 985-1938
www.p1aquax.com/Race-info/Key%20West/2017/84228

Experience non-stop racing action as Sea-Doo, Yamaha, and Kawasaki personal watercraft racers take to the water averaging 75 mph. This race is the final round in 2017 and serves as the overall championship for the PRO Enduro and International Amateur Championship. Jetcross Jet Ski stand up races will also be a part of this family friendly event free to the public.

Dec. 31, 2017 Location: Key West
New Year's Eve Shoe Drop Celebration
www.mallorysquare.com/new-years-eve-in-key-west

Ring in the New Year in Key West fashion with one of three ball drops in Old Town. Watch the pirate wench drop from the top of a sail boat with live music and festivities at the Schooner Wharf bar on the Historic Key West Waterfront. There are two places to watch the drop on Duval Street. The most popular and largest crowd can be found at Sloppy Joes who lowers a Conch Shell to ring in the New Year. The other possibility is to see Sushi drop from the balcony in a larger than life red high heel shoe at New Orleans House.

Key West

FAMOUS
KEY WEST HOMES

Famous Key West Homes

Key West has had more than its fair share of famous residents over the years. In its beginnings Key West was a wrecker's and pirate's town. It became a very affluent community by salvaging the cargo of ships that became lodged on its coral reefs off shore. In the days of Ernest Hemingway in the late 1920s it was a mecca for artists, writers, and other creative souls. In the 1970's Jimmy Buffett gave his musical career a jump start when he left Nashville and came to Key West with the help of his good friend Jerry Jeff Walker. Paraphrasing Jimmy when he first came to town, and asked about the music scene at the time, "he was the music scene." No one was really performing a lot of live music as they do all over the island now. In these next pages, you will see some of the homes that belonged to these famous residents and find out a little more about the people who have called Key West home.

TREV/MOR APARTMENTS

314 Simonton Street

In 1928 when Ernest and Pauline Hemingway came to Key West, they had intended to stay just long enough to pick up a new Ford automobile from the Trevor/Morris Ford dealership and drive first to Arkansas then to Kansas where they had planned to give birth to their first child, Patrick. The new car was a wedding gift from Pauline's Uncle Gus Pfeiffer. However, the car was delayed for 6 weeks and as a way to make up for this the Ford dealer agreed to house the Hemingways in an upstairs apartment over their car showroom. Ernest used this time to work on A Farewell to Arms and also make new friends who helped him take advantage of the excellent salt water fishing of the surrounding waters.

907 WHITEHEAD STREET

Ernest Hemingway Home

After renting homes in Key West every winter from 1928 to 1931, the Hemingways bought and renovated this home in April 1931. This Spanish Colonial home with its wide covered porches and long shuttered windows was originally built in 1851 by the marine architect and wrecker Asa Tift. During its day it was one of the first homes on the island to have indoor plumbing and also had the only swimming pool within 100 miles. The massive swimming pool was built on the site of Ernest's former boxing ring in the backyard and cost over $20,000 to construct. Built during during his absence it is legend that when he returned to find out the cost of the work , Ernest gave Pauline his "last penny" which is encased in the cement at the edge of the pool to this day. Hemingway wrote many of his best works in his second floor studio out back including A Farewell to Arms, Green Hills of Africa, To Have and Have Not, and For Whom the Bell Tolls. This beautiful home at 907 Whitehead served as the home of Ernest Hemingway until he and Pauline divorced in 1940 and he moved to Cuba where he lived in his estate, Finca Vigia.

1431 Duncan Street

Tennessee Williams Home

Located on a quiet corner lot at 1431 Duncan Street you'll find the quaint but unassuming former home of two time Pulitzer Prize winning playwright and author, Tennessee Williams. This attractive white clapboard Bahamian style home can be seen peeking out from behind a large traveler's palm and other assorted greenery without fanfare to announce its colorful previous owner. Tennessee Williams first came to Key West in 1941 at the age of thirty and spent his first years in the Southernmost City living in a boarding house and hotels. It is popularly thought that he wrote a draft of "A Streetcar Named Desire" at the La Concha Hotel on Duval Street. In 1950 he bought this home on Duncan Street and created his own compound composed of the main house, guest cottage, swimming pool, and a one-room writing studio which he called the "Mad House." Although he had his own pool it is said that he loved to go to South Beach every day for a swim.

In researching this chapter I found out that Tennessee Williams was a painter as well as a writer. As his career as a popular playwright was on the wane he started to paint in the 1960's. In a recent article by Key West Citizen columnist and author, Mandy Miles, I found out several things in fact in her interview with longtime resident and close friend of Williams, David Wolkowsky. Wolksowsky stated that "Tennessee would write in the morning and paint in the afternoon." In my mind when I hear the name Tennessee Williams an image comes to mind of a photo I have seen of him in his heyday with his entourage surrounding him, drink in hand, with his head thrown back laughing with a huge grin on his face. However, there was another side to this multifaceted man. According to Wolkowsky, "He was very generous in quiet ways, always helping people without wanting credit for it." He could be seen around town on his bicycle and to those that really knew him was known simply as Tom. Today the former Tennessee Williams home is a fully renovated private home so please don't knock on the front door asking to see the famous former Key West's playwright and bon vivant's house.

1421 DUNCAN STREET

Rose Tattoo

This home is located next to the former Tennessee Williams home on Duncan Street and was featured in the Academy Award winning 1955 film "The Rose Tatoo." The location company decided to produce much of the film based on a Tennessee Williams play in Key West and filmed many scenes at this home at 1421 Duncan Street. Featuring Burt Lancaster and Anna Magnani, The Rose Tattoo is the story of a widowed Sicilian woman in the American South who is devastated by the death of her husband in a tragic accident. She withdraws from life into her grief but is later shocked by her late husband's infidelities. Just as she is reeling from these revelations, a new man enters her world and offers her opportunity for renewed love.

This beautiful home was purchased and lovingly renovated by a couple who love Key West as well as the actress Anna Magnani who was featured in A Rose Tattoo. It had fallen into a state of disrepair over the years but was purchased and resurrected by Robin and Carla Gay when they noticed that it came on the market in 2012. They used movie stills and a team of architects to painstakingly return to its previous beauty as portrayed in the award winning movie. Once again this is a private home today so please respect the owner's privacy.

704 WADDELL AVENUE

Jimmy Buffett's Apartment

When Jimmy Buffett sang about stumbling over to Louie's Backyard he didn't have far to go. His apartment was upstairs in this former apartment complex which is now part of the Coconut Resort.

Photo by Mark Lee.

2505 SEIDENBERG

Tom Corcoran

Tom Corcoran had the perfect job to meet and entertain many of Key West's residents and tourists in the early 1970's. He was the bartender at the Chart Room on the Key West waterfront where pretty much anyone who was anybody came to quench their thirst. It was just such a day when Jerry Jeff Walker came in and introduced Tom to a friend of his that was seeking refuge from the Nashville life and was looking to start over. This young man's name was Jimmy Buffett. Yes, Jimmy Buffett was served his first beer in Key West at the Chart Room by none other than Tom Corcoran. From that first meeting they formed a long friendship which has given Corcoran the chance to make many contributions to Jimmy's music in the form of song lyrics and album covers. You may not know that Tom contributed to both the songs " A Cuban Crime of Passion" and "Fins."

Key West

WHAT TO DO

FISHING

Fish Monster Charters
700 Front Street
Key West, Florida
(305)-432-0046
www.fishmonstercharters.com

For a genuine Keys fishing experience and a trip that you won't soon forget, you need to get in touch with Fish Monster Charters and Captain Marlin Scott. Captain Scott is the best ambassador that I know for Key West and The Florida Keys and does a great job of making folks feel welcome and comfortable on their fishing expedition. Whether you're a first timer or a repeat customer, which he has a lot of, you will have a great time out on the water with him and his crew.

Fish Monster has been running charters for more than ten years and is based out of the A & B Marina on the Key West Waterfront. They have two impeccably maintained 36 foot Luhrs Tournament Express boats, The Premium Time and Reel Deal, which they use in the business and offer a variety of trips. Check out the website to see what suits your needs best.

The catch depends on the time of the year and what is biting at the time. At the moment that I am writing this, the dolphin are really tearing it up and when they return to dock I have seen them literally fill up a deck cart with these colorful and tasty local gamefish. If you want to see for yourself before you come down check out their daily Facebook posts on the Fish Monster Magazine page where you can see them in action.

For an extra special adventure, take the overnight trip out to the Dry Tortugas. This once in a lifetime experience can be for up to four people and includes a day of fishing as well as some well-earned relaxation as the sun goes down over this remote tropical island. After a grilled dinner of your day's catch, you get to sleep onboard the boat anchored in the harbor at historic Fort Jefferson. If you would like to explore the fort or do some snorkeling this is also a possibility. You

don't have to take just my word for it. All you have to do is read some
of the glowing reviews from their satisfied customers to see that Fish
Monster Charters is first class. I highly recommend them for an unforgettable Florida Keys fishing experience.

Big Kahuna Charters
Florida Keys
Tel: (305) 304-5498
www.bigkahunacharters.net

Captain Chris Robinson is a long time Key Wester and you'll have to
search far and wide to find a captain who is more experienced than he.
Captain Chris has over 40 years' experience fishing the waters of the
Keys and specializes in flats fishing for permit, bonefish, tarpon, bar-
racuda, shark, and cobia. Originally from St. Augustine, Florida, Chris
moved to Key West in the 1970s and was one of the best bartenders
around working at The Chart Room and later the Afterdeck at Louie's
Backyard. He hung out with friends like the struggling singer at the
time, Jimmy Buffett and journalist Hunter S. Thompson in his off
time. After some years as a part time bartender and fishing guide, he
decided to make it a full-time pursuit in 2004. Chris is comfortable taking the novice or expert angler out and strives to give you "the time of
your life" in the backcountry and flats of some of the most beautiful
areas that you will ever see.

Southpaw Fishing
5950 Peninsular Avenue
Phone: 305-393-2306
www.southpawfishingkeywest.com

If you sail with Captain Brad Simonds aboard the 43-foot custom built
Torres sportfisherman named the Southpaw, you will be getting both
an award winning and Orvis endorsed fishing guide. He has over 30

years of fishing experience in the Florida Keys and started his career after college at the venerable Bud and Mary's in Islamorada back in the early 80s. He is dedicated to providing you with the best possible fishing experience and draws on his many skills to put you on the fish. His vessel is one of the cleanest and newest and one of the few to offer a tuna tower. This gives him an advantage in peering down into the water and spotting the signs in the water in pursuit of the wily game fish of the day. His boat is impeccably maintained and is equipped with the latest in electronics for navigation and safety. Try Captain Brad and the Southpaw for your next fishing trip and see what sets them apart from the rest.

Linda D Sportfishing
1801 North Roosevelt Blvd,
Key West Charter Boat Row, Dock 19 & 20,
Phone: 800-299-9798
Cellular: 305-304-8102

To say that fishing runs in their blood is very true statement for the Wickers family that have run Linda D Sportfishing in Key West Florida for almost 80 years. Indeed Captain Billy Wickers III is the fourth generation to Captain and guide these waters. His list of awards and prizes for fishing tournaments is too long to list here, but check the website. Linda D Fishing is a holder of the Trip Advisor excellence award and is here to provide the best possible trip for its customers. They offer ½, ¾, and full day charters and go out for a variety of different fish. They have hosted former Florida Governor Jeb Bush and other high profile celebrity guests and would love to have you fish with them as well. Call or email them today for information on setting up your next fishing trip in Key West.

Dream Catcher Charters Inc.
5555 College Road
(305)-292-7212
www.dreamcatchercharters.com

Dream Catcher Charters is another 2016 recipient of the Trip Advisor award of excellence. Their website describes their staff as a "team of professionals who have a common goal of showing people an amazing time on the waters of Key West on fishing, boating, sightseeing, and snorkeling charters." They proudly proclaim that their boats and fishing gear are in tip top shape and well maintained and all customers are treated as friends or family. Each year their boats are either updated or sold so their crafts are always in like new or new condition. They also have the best in fishing gear to provide you to catch more fish. They have managed to grow every year by pioneering many of the customer service standards used by the competition today.

If you want to fish with one of the best and the innovators of Key West Fishing guides, contact Dream Catchers.

JETSKI RENTAL

Fury Water Adventures of Key West
241 Front Street
(855) 990-0197
www.furycat.com

Fury Watersports is your one stop shop all of your watersports activities in Key West. They have three locations to serve you and have been in business for almost 30 years. One of the great things that they offer is a 90 minute jet ski tour of Key West. It is a 28 mile tour all on water and you get to see the island from a different point of view. They use only the best of equipment which is Sea Doo 3 seat jet ski which is known for giving a smooth, stable ride. Not only will you see points of interest such as Mallory Square and the Southernmost Point, but also the beautiful back country and remote islands surrounding Key West. One of the highlights of the tour is the chance to stop on a sandbar, check things out, and take a swim. If you have limited boating experience, don't let that stop you as their tours can accommodate the beginning or expert jet skier. Just call or go to their website to get started.

Jet skiers play off Smathers Beach. Photo by Mark Lee.

Sunset Watersports
201 William Street
Reservation (855) 378-6386 or online
www.sunsetwatersportskeywest.com

Sunset Sports offers a ton of different activities on the water, but their Waverunner rentals are done from Parrot Key Resort on North Roosevelt. They have a 1 ½ hour tour that includes a 25 mile ride all the way around the island of Key West. You'll see some of Key West's most beautiful scenery and iconic sites including the Southernmost Point, Key West Harbour, and more. You'll find that their prices are reasonable and they always have new equipment. They start with new Yamaha Waverunners every season and you don't pay extra for gas or the 2nd rider. It's included in the price that you pay. You can reserve your excursion either online or by calling their number above.

Barefoot Billy's
(305) 900-3088
www.barefootbillys.com

For over twenty years Barefoot Billy's has been a leader in Jet Ski tours and recreational equipment rental in Key West. They have two beachfront locations, the Casa Marina Resort and the Reach Resort, to get you out on the water having fun. Their "world famous" Jet Ski tour lasts around two hours and encompasses a 27 mile circuit that winds around the island and back and forth between the Gulf of Mexico and the Atlantic Ocean. If you're the independent type and feel like riding in an unstructured environment, they also rent jet skis by the hour. Jet Ski rental is but one of the many activities that they offer. For more info check their website and get going today. Also if you book a tour online you can save 10% by using the coupon code BAREFOOT.

Island Safari Tours
5016 5th Avenue (Stock Island)
Tel: 305-879-2124
www.islandsafaritourskeywest.com

You'll find Island Safari Tours just over the Cow Channel Bridge in Stock Island, Key West's quieter neighbor to the east. Their tour guides are chosen for their knowledge and skills on the sea and will take you on intriguing two hour, 27-mile journey around Key West. You'll have four stops on the tour to give you a chance to catch your breath or have questions answered by their expert staff. They also offer lots of other activities on the water such as parasailing, snorkeling, and kayaking. For those land lubbers they offer such things as scooter, bike, and electric car rentals. You'll find that their prices are reasonable and they're easy to find.

SAILING CRUISES

Danger Charters
Docked at the Margaritaville Resort Marina
255 Front Street
Book online or call (305) 304-7999
www.dangercharters.com

Danger Charters is consistently rated as one of the top tour companies in Key West and their Wind and Wine Sail was named by Coastal Living Magazine as one of the top two Sunset Sails in North America. On this scenic sunset sail they serve eight different wines sourced from around the world and pair it with a variety of appetizers including Havarti Dill, Smoke Gouda and Summer Sausage, Caprese Skewers, Water Crackers with Brie, Green Apple with a Honey Drizzle, and more. Sit back and relax and watch the crew do their work as they hoist the sails on the 65 foot schooner. All you have to do is take it easy, enjoy the music and refreshments, and watch for the green flash as the sun sets in the West. They also offer other excursions so check their website to explore all of the possibilities.

The Jolly II Rover
Elizabeth Street, Key West, FL 33040
(305) 304-2235
www.schoonerjollyrover.com

Travel back to Key West's early pirate days aboard the classic 80-foot square rigged topsail schooner, The Jolly Rover II and have your own swashbuckling experience aboard Key West's "most photographed ship." It plies the beautiful green waters around CayoHueso resplendent with its signature red sails furled in the tropical winds. The Jolly Rover II is a Certificate of Excellence recipient from Trip Advisor and its website boasts hundreds of satisfied customers with glowing reviews. The two-hour sunset cruises are a treat for the senses with stimulations for sight and sound. The palate of color on fire with the Key West sunset serves as a brilliant backdrop as cannons fire and you get to take a turn at the ships wheel charting your course around the island. You'll find an authentic old world sailing experience aboard the Jolly Rover II and make memories to last a lifetime.

Sunset sailing adventure with Fury Watersports. Photo by Mark Lee.

Breezin Charters
Key West Bight Marina, Slip E-7
207 William Street
(305) 797-1561
www.breezincharters.com

Join the highly qualified and experienced Captain Dees and sail the tropical waters of Key West on his 42-foot Catalina sailboat. Captain Dees has been sailing charters for over 20 years and has been using his graceful boat Breezin since 2003. He is a two time Trip Advisor Award of Excellence recipient and will give you a nautical experience to re-member. You can learn the basics of sailing with Captain Dees as he offers lessons. He also offers a 4-hour and 7-hour charter perfect for relaxing on the water and catching a little snorkeling time out on the reefs. You could choose to take a sunset cruise and watch for the green flash as the sun slowly sinks into the western ocean. If you're thinking about celebrating a special occasion, why not have that wedding, birthday, or anniversary aboard the Breezing with Captain Dees at the helm helping to create that perfect memory that you will treasure for a lifetime. For rates and reservations, check out his website and get ready to set sail.

MORE SAILING RESOURCES

Schooner Spirit of Independence
202 William Street
(305)-849-4032
www.schoonerspiritofindependence.com

Catamaran Echo
611 Grinnell Street
Historic Seaport, Pier D, Key West
(305) 292-5044
www.dolphinecho.com

Tortuga Sailing Adventures
Private Yacht Charters & Overnight Getaways
7005 Shrimp Road, Dock A-6, Key West
(305) 896-2477
www.tortugasailingadventures.com

Scooter Rentals

Sun Shine Scooters
1910 North Roosevelt Boulevard
(305) 294-9990
www.sunshinescootersinc.com

Tropical Rentals
1300 Duval Street
(305) 294-8136
www.tropicalrentacar.com

The Moped Hospital
601 Truman Avenue
(305) 292-7679
www.mopedhospital.com

A & M Rentals
523 Truman Avenue
(305)-896-1921
www.amscooterskeywest.com

Pirate Rentals
401 Southard Street
877-PIRATE-6 or 305 295-0000
www.piratescooterrentals.com

SNORKEL TRIPS

Floridays

601 Front Street, Hyatt Resort and Spa

Key West, FL 33040

(305) 744-8335

www.floridayskeywest.com

Sebago Watersports-Key West

Key West Historic Seaport

205 Elizabeth Street, Unit I

Key West, FL 33040

800-507-9955

www.sebagokeywest.com

Fury Water Adventures-Key West

2 Duval Street

Key West, FL 33040

(855) 831-5997

www.furycat.com/key-west/snorkeling

PADDLE BOARDING

Lazy Dog Adventures
5114 Overseas Hwy, Key West, FL 33040
(305) 295-9898
www.lazydog.com

SUP Key West
5001 5th Ave, Key West, FL 33040
(305) 240-1426
www.supkeywest.com

Nomadic SUP Paddleboard Eco Tours
Key West, FL, 33040
(305)-395-9494
www.nomadicsup.com

KEY WEST ON A BUDGET

Key West is one of the most laid back, breathtaking places you'll ever go in the continental US. It's also this very thing that makes it so attractive to a lot of different people. It is one of the most popular stops for many cruise ship itineraries and also attracts a lot of wealthy people with the means to get away from the real world to play. The other side of this is Key West is not a cheap place to live or play. However, through my time that I've spent here I'm going to pass on some of the tips that I've picked up to save you a little money and stretch your travel dollar as much as you can.

The first thing you need to know is there are defined travel seasons in Key West. The high season here is the polar opposite of most coastal destinations. Because of the mild temperate climate in the winter, snow birds flock to South Florida in the winter to escape the freezing temps and icy conditions back at home. The least expensive time to come to Key West is generally considered to be between June and November or the "off season." Personally my favorite time to go to the Keys is November due to the lack of humidity and abundant sun and warm temps. It feels like late Spring/Early Summer most days and the humidity is long gone by then. My wife and I have even tent camped this time of year at our favorite waterfront campsite in Boyd's Campground with a sunrise view that has yet to be equaled by any conventional room that we've found. Barring any special events that may be happening during the off season you'll find that rooms are more plentiful and the prices are lower during this time.

Your lodging can be the most expensive part of your stay as many of the waterfront resorts start in the $300 to $400 per night range and go up from there. Depending on your tastes I have found a couple of ways to spend the night in Key West for under $100 dollars a night and no it doesn't involve sleeping on a park bench or under a bridge.

The first involves camping out and enjoying the great outdoors. There are several campgrounds in Key West, but my personal favorite is Boyd's. It's just across the Cow Key Channel Bridge on Stock Island and offers a variety of campsites to suit any budget. Inland campsites start at $58 in the off season and $66 in season. There is also a mix of RV as well as tent campers here and although there are both inland and waterfront campsites, you're never far away from the water in this well-kept and impeccably managed facility. It has spotless bathroom and shower facilities and has an onsite laundry for your convenience. Lots of extras including free Wi-Fi, a heated swimming pool, and boat ramp and docks make this an attractive choice if you're the outdoor type and looking for a less expensive way to experience the Keys. Check out their website at www.boydscampground.com for more details and reserve your site.

Another way to save on accommodations is to stay at one of my other go to lodging choices which is the Key West Bed and Breakfast on Williams Street in Key West. It's located in a quiet residential area in Old Town and is a short walk to the Historic Key West Seaport. The Key West Bed and Breakfast is an attractive two story home with both first and second story covered porches. Residents are free to lounge on either porch and relax and enjoy the peaceful atmosphere.

They have a library of books that can be borrowed and I made sure to leave them a complimentary copy of my book during my last stay. Breakfast is served every morning and consists of fresh breads and fruits sourced from local areas. A typical mix of fruits may be papaya, melon, pineapple, plums, pears, or whatever is in season. Room prices range in the summer from $99 to $175 and in the winter from $125 to $ 285. There are both rooms that share baths as well as those that have a private bath. This hotel came highly recommended from one of my friends in Key West and it did not disappoint. I hope you have a chance to check it out and enjoy it as much as I do. Here's their website, www.keywestbandb.com.

Yet another way to save is by reading the local newspaper, The Key West Citizen, due to the ads that restaurants run touting their specials this time of year. I ate at one of my favorite restaurants, Pepe's, in June

2016 and used a 50 percent off entrée coupon to have a great steak dinner for well under twenty dollars. This summer they are running a summer three course dinner special for $25 which includes appetizer, entrée, and dessert. These are just a couple of examples of how it definitely pays to read the paper. Other restaurants run daily specials during the off season to attract business due to the slowdown in tourism and to cater to the locals. During the off season, it's also noticeably easier to get a table in my favorite places due to the decreased tourist traffic which is just another benefit of traveling in the off season.

If you're a coupon user then you may want to check out some of the free website coupons that are available at www.keywestchamber.org, www.keyscashsaver.com, or www.keyscoupons.com. All of these coupons can be printed and used at the business, no hassle. They can save you money on a lot of different things such as activities, tours, transportation, food, drinks, and a lot more. There are also a couple of discount cards that you can purchased prior to your trip. They are the Key West Vacation Pass and the Key West Bar Card. The Key West vacation pass has a ton of "BOGO" offers and promises to savings of over 850 dollars. It has a variety of two for one offers on anything from a tour of the Curry Mansion to a Snorkel or Sunset cruise aboard a large catamaran. The Key West Bar Card entitles you to a two for one drink every day for a year at 14 of Key West finest bars. Yes, you heard correctly for a whole year. That's over 4800 free drinks in a years' time. Likewise, they also offer a couple more cards which are the Restaurant Card and Backstage Card. The Restaurant card saves you 10% off your meal at 17 eateries across Key West and Stock Island. The Backstage Card saves you 15% off your cost at a dozen businesses that provide tours, fishing, scooter rentals, and the like. These for purchase discounts can be found at keywestvacationpass.com and keywestbarcard.com.

There's now a phone app called Free Libations that allows you to buy a drink and get a free one just like happy hour without the time constraints. At this time, there are six bars on the island that will allow you to buy one and get one free per person per day with a Facebook checkin.

Just download the app to your phone and start using it. For more details you can go to www.freelibations.com.

Later in the book I'll also give you a few of my favorites that I come back to time after time when I'm in Key West which I have found to be my go to places for the best food, tours, and transportation. For now here are a few absolutely free activities that are also some of my top ten choices to do in Key West:

1. Visit the Southernmost Point and have your picture taken at the most photographed place in town. Cuba is a short 90 miles to the South from here.

2. Go to the Mallory Square Sunset Celebration. A longstanding Key West tradition, it's not just a place it is more like a cool, quirky sideshow on the waterfront complete with street performers, food vendors, and artisans. Come early and take it all in.

3. Wander the Key West Cemetery and read the epitaphs on the whitewashed above ground tombs. Many of the tombs carry witty as well as downright laughable messages such as the one on the tomb of B. P. Roberts, "I told you I was sick."

4. Take another photo at the iconic Mile Marker 0 on Whitehead Street. This marks the end of U.S. Highway 1 that runs from Fort Kent, Maine to Key West, Florida.

5. Check out the Florida Keys Eco-Discovery Center where you can learn about the plants and animals that are native to the land and water of the Florida Keys. This center of discovery is housed in an over 6000 square foot facility that encourages and enables interactive learning activities and features the Aquarius, a mock-up of the world's only underwater ocean laboratory.

MARK'S PERSONAL PICKS

I get friends asking me all the time where to stay or eat and what to do in Key West. This chapter gives you some advice on some of my personal recommendations. This is the same advice I give my friends and some of the places that I like to go. I've sent quite a few friends down to Key West and one couple in particular comes to mind that went this past summer. My friend Wanda said that she and her husband used my book the whole trip and t the only time that they went somewhere that I had not recommended they were disappointed. I consider that quite a complement and it is the result of the thoroughness in my research by actually traveling to and checking out the places that I recommend. Not to say that I have picked the only places in Key West that are good and all the rest are bad. They just happened to pick somewhere that was not on my list and were disappointed. There are tons of places to eat and stay in Key West and I don't list them all, but you can count on if it's in my book that I have some experience there and in my opinion I would return there again based on that experience.

ACCOMMODATIONS

The first thing you should know is that Key West hotels comes in all price ranges and depending upon the time of year and what events are going on you can spend a lot for a place to stay. I am going to give you a few tips from the budget to luxury and a few in between. Let your budget be your guide as all of these places are clean, well-staffed, and accommodating.

KEY WEST BED AND BREAKFAST

415 William Street
Key West, FL
(305) 296-7274
www.keywestbandb.com

I first stayed in the Key West Bed and Breakfast this past June for a few days and was delighted by several things. First, of course, was its very reasonable price. Unlike most beach or coastal communities summer is the slow season in Key West and the most reasonable time to find a hotel room. I stayed for around 80 dollars a night in a cozy upstairs room which had a twin bed and a chair plus chest of drawers and closet for my clothes. Just outside my door was a long covered porch which spanned the width of the front of the house. It had chairs and tables plus a woven hammock, perfect for afternoon napping.

Second was the fact that they serve breakfast every morning using fresh fruits that are in season plus home baked goods and fresh bagels and bread. This is served daily from 8:30 a.m. till 10:30 a.m. Although they allow no cooking in the kitchen by the guests, you do have use of the refrigerator to store food or drink that you may bring home. You can walk to any number of restaurants in the area for lunch or dinner.

Third it has a secluded fenced back yard with a small dipping pool to cool off in and also a patio with table and chairs to enjoy the outdoors. You'll find the Key West Bed and Breakfast tucked away in a quiet Old Town residential area on Williams Street. This B and B is a great place to stay due to price, location, and its wonderful staff. It's within easy walking distance of Duval Street and the Historic Key West Sea Port.

The Inn at Key West

3420 N Roosevelt Blvd,
Key West, FL 33040
(305) 294-5541
www.theinnatkeywest.com

When I drove up to the Inn at Key West it looked nice and inviting. The lobby is large and open to the second floor of the hotel. There is a seating area in the spacious waiting area as well as a concierge that is on duty to help with local suggestions for excursions, dining, and the like. The front desk staff are very friendly and eager to please. Our room was on the back of the facility without much of a view, but they do have rooms around the pool as well as balcony rooms that overlook Roosevelt Boulevard and the bay. The bathroom is ample and has a large wooden cabinet in which you can store your clothes and a room safe for valuables.

The fresh water pool is huge and is surrounded by tall green coconut palms which sway in the warm gentle breezes. There is rock formation waterfall at the far end of the pool and plenty of lounge chairs in which to enjoy the tropical rays of the sun. You'll find the Oasis Tiki Bar, open from 10 a.m. till 11 p.m., next to what their website boasts is Key West's largest pool. There is an onsite restaurant, but you will also find the IHOP next door and it's a short distance down the street to the Stoned Crab or Outback Steaks.

SOUTHERNMOST HOUSE

1400 Duval Street
Key West, FL
(305) 296-3141
www.southernmosthouse.com

The Southernmost House is an elegant boutique hotel which once served as the one bedroom mansion of one of Key West's well to do families. This oceanfront mansion located at the corner of Duval and South streets has one of the most enviable locations on the entire island and there are 18 luxuriously well-appointed guest rooms on the property. This is the quiet end of Duval Street which is blocks away from the boisterous bar scene that most equate Key West with. Across the street you can see The Southernmost Café and South Beach. South Beach is a small, but scenic inlet where you can take a quick dip in the warm clear Atlantic waters and soak up the sun in one its comfy lounge chairs for rent. It is said that the famous playwright and former Key West resident, Tennessee Williams swam almost daily at this beach.

On our most recent stay, we found our room to be spacious and comfortable with its oversized king size planter style bed, adjacent sitting area with refrigerator and private bathroom with a walk-in shower room. We particularly enjoyed the heated pool and the thought that we were swimming outside in November. This was a feat we would not attempt in our pool at home this time of year. As we stepped into the pool area we were treated to a grand vista of towering date palm trees supported by a backdrop of the Atlantic Ocean lapping at the shore just a few feet away. The view from the pool must be appreciated in person and I liked it so much I had one of our photos of it enlarged and it hangs in the den of our home.

Carl, the bartender, haled from Eastern Europe and was there to serve up whatever tropical drink you could think of. He, as was all the other staff, were super friendly and played a part in a long list of pluses that we loved about staying at this property. This hotel ranks towards the top of our list as one of our all-time favorites.

Looking towards the pool from the seawall at The Southernmost House. Photo by Mark Lee.

Casa Marina

1500 Reynolds Street
Key West, FL
(305) 296-3535
www.casamarinaresort.com

The Casa Marina is one of Key West's premier luxury resorts located on the Atlantic Ocean side of the island. It was originally constructed by the builder of the Overseas Railway, Henry Flagler, and opened in 1920. It was constructed at that time to give his wealthy passengers and railroad guests somewhere to stay after they had travelled to the end of the line on his "Train to Paradise." It is built rock solid and is constructed of the same heavy duty imported cement that his railroad supports were made of and has a foundation which is 22 inches thick. The hotel property was designed by the architects who also designed the New York Metropolitan Opera,

New York Public Library, and the Senate and House of Representatives office buildings in Washington, DC. Its lobby has tall stately ceilings with exposed wooden supports and dark rich wooden floors. It also offers plush comfortable seating areas with both chairs and sofas throughout.

Just a few days after it had opened on New Year's Eve 1920, it played host to President Warren G. Harding. It has not only served as a hotel, but during the 1940s it was purchased by the Navy and was used to house officers during World War II. As the war drew to a close it was reopened as a hotel and played host to a number of celebrities and movie stars. Once more during the Cuban missile crisis of 1962, it was leased by the military and housed Army missile crews sent to protect the United States in case of an attack from the South.

Today after a 43-million-dollar renovation, the Casa Marina Resort is a 5-star luxury resort and is part of the Waldorf Astoria Hotels organization. It shines as it first did with its original luxurious luster and each if its 311 comfortable rooms offer such amenities as LCD Flat panel TV, clock with MP3 connector, refrigerator, coffee maker, and local newspaper delivery every week day.

The back of the property is a virtual oasis and offers not one but two large swimming pools surrounded by towering coconut palms. If you get hungry you can order from the outside restaurant and dine pool or beachside. It also offers what may be the islands largest private beach where you can lounge on one of the many reclining chairs under swaying palms and soak up some warm tropical sun. If water sports are your game there is a vendor ready to set you up with any number of high seas activities such as Jet Skis, Sailboats, or water cycles.

My wife and I look forward to coming to the Casa every November as we and several thousand other Parrot Heads flock to Key West for Meeting of the Minds. This is what originally brought us to the Casa Marina and after just one visit we were hooked. We would highly recommend staying here for the view, amenities, and the wonderful staff.

THE SPEAKEASY INN

1117 Duval Street
Key West, FL
(305) 296-2680
www.speakeasyinn.com

I certainly don't want to leave this gem of an inn out of my personal recommendations. I stayed here last summer and was really impressed. The bed and breakfast that I was staying at couldn't accommodate my entire stay so I spent my last night here at the Speakeasy. I thought that I would have to pay more for this kind of room on Duval Street, but that was not the case. I got a King room with refrigerator and bathroom with a spacious walk-in shower for mid $130's per night. Keep in mind that summer is the low season, but there are times that the rates may go as low as $109. In the high season, during the winter and spring break, rates may go as high as $259 which is still extremely reasonable for a room in Key West, especially with this good location.

The Speakeasy is the former home of Raul Vaquez who was a cigar selector at the Gato cigar factory. Raul was a hard working entrepreneur in Key West and also carried on a bustling import business. He was a Rum runner and brought in illegal liquor by boat from Cuba during the prohibition. Like most business men, he used advertising to boost his business, but his was more discreet than most other club owners who offered liquor and gambling. Instead of posting an ad in the local paper stating "Club in Rear," he used the gingerbread trim between the balustrades of his porches on his home to do this. If you look closely today you can see the outline of liquor and wine bottles carved into the woodwork. There are also hearts, diamonds, clubs, and spades representing card suits announcing that gambling was available.

The rooms are extremely clean, the staff is friendly, and there is a rum bar in the lobby open from 11 a.m. till 11 p.m. You can relax with a drink out front on the porch and people watch all the sights and sounds of Duval Street. This inn was an excellent find.

Great coffee at the Key West waterfront. Photo by Mark Lee.

Restaurants

I have a handful of go to spots in town when I want to go out for food which is most of the time because we usually don't stay anywhere that allows cooking. It just depends on the time of day and what I'm in the mood for. I'll lay out some of our favorites by category and give you a little detail about why we like each place so much.

Breakfast

PEPE'S

Pepe's is stated to be the oldest restaurant in town and has one of the best breakfasts also. We like to sit at the bar in the open air brick paved patio and have our breakfast al fresco as we catch up on all of the local news from our friendly neighborhood bartenders and the folks on both sides of us. You never know who you may meet sitting next to here. One day we were sitting beside a NASCAR marketing exec and the next day were talking to a guy that comes down every winter and rents a house to get away from the wintry Northern weather. I like the two eggs special with a meat and the bread of the day. My wife like the chipped beef on toast. You may know it by another name, SOS! We also both recommend either the mimosa or screwdriver because they're both made with fresh squeezed orange juice. The Bloody Mary was also tasty as they make their own mix from scratch. We liked the coffee so much we took a couple of pounds back with us.

SUNSHINE GRILL

Chris Itrato and his wife Noelle, two of the nicest people you'll ever meet, run this cool diner on White Street. I had emailed Noelle after a super delicious breakfast that I had there last summer and let her know

I would like to include them in my next guide book. Then I actually had the chance to meet and sit down with Chris in November. I really like these folks who both come from a Disney background and it shows. Their attention to detail is outstanding and they serve up great food with impeccable service in a kind of funky fifties diner motif. I've only eaten breakfast there, but the rest of the menu looks really good. Their sausage biscuits and gravy is considered one of their specialties and is quite good. I look forward to seeing them again in a few months. You'll find that White Street is a bit outside of the tourist belt of Key West so stop in and dine like a local with the Itratos. It's across the street from Faustos.

CUBAN COFFEE WITH BREAKFAST

CUBAN COFFEE QUEEN

I like the Cuban Coffee Queen because it combines two of my favorites things, morning coffee and waterfront living. It is directly adjacent to the Key West Seaport and I like to take my coffee and walk the docks checking out all of the boats that are tied up in the marina. Their Cuban Coffee is really good and they also make a mean breakfast sandwich. One of the best places in town to get your morning started.

FIVE BROTHERS GROCERY

This little bodega has been serving up Cuban coffee and conversation since the 1970s. It is the nerve center of the Old Town neighborhood which surrounds it at the corner of Southard and Grinnell Streets. You'll find locals sipping small cups of Cuban coffee, munching on some delicious handmade breakfast sandwiches, and sharing the news of the day. It's open from 6:30 a.m. till 3:00 p.m. every day, but Sunday. Hey, everybody needs a day off.

LUNCH

JACK FLATS

This sports bar on Duval Street is known for its 19 big screen TV's and its food portions that are almost as large. It's become a tradition for us to go watch college football when we're in town in the fall and have lunch. I like the club sandwich and tater tots which is so much food my wife and I can usually share it. We also like the buffalo shrimp, fish sandwich, and Buffalo Chicken Wrap. The beer is cold and the drinks are good. Sports fan's paradise and easy on the wallet.

EL SIBONEY

This is the best authentic Cuban sit down restaurant in town. It's in a little brick building tucked away in an Old Town residential area. No frills except for the food which is out of this world good. It is known for its ample portions and good service. One tip though is it can get busy at times so you may have to wait, but is should be worth it.

SANDY'S

I could have just as easily put Sandy's in the Cuban coffee category, but I usually go here for the Cuban mix sandwich. I credit one of their signature sandwiches for nursing me back to health after a particularly trying Thursday night after the Jimmy Buffett concert. One of their Cuban sandwiches, a Pepsi, and a few fries and I was good as new. If you're going to eat it there they do have a few barstools and table top outside, but no inside dining area. My go to place for my Cuban or Media Noche fix. They're open every day from 5 a.m. till midnight. Yes the Cuban coffee and breakfast sandwiches are great also.

SEAFOOD

HOGFISH BAR AND GRILL

A couple of tips about this real deal seafood hide out on Stock Island. This is where you go to see how Key West used to be back in the day. No frills, lots of fresh and tasty seafood and fish. Hard to find, yes, but if you can follow the little yellow signs or use a GPS you can find this jewel sitting on the shore of Safe Harbor Marina. Legend has it that the Bay of Pigs Invasion was planned and launched from this location. We like to sit out at the picnic tables which are literally side to side with the boats docked a few feet away. I recommend the Hogfish, duh, and the Key West Pink Shrimp.

HALF SHELL RAW BAR

Pat Croce's long time seafood restaurant sits waterfront directly on the Historic Key West Seaport. Surrounded by the fishing fleet of Key West, the fresh seafood flows in daily and they own their own seafood market so you know you're getting the freshest. Kenny Chesney used the bar as a backdrop for one of his hit songs, *When I See This Bar*! Some of their specialties are broiled garlic oysters, a basket of fish and chips, steamed middle neck clams, chilled Key West peel and eat shrimp, and conch ceviche.

EATON STREET SEAFOOD MARKET

Until recently this Old Town market just sold fresh seafood to take home and cook, but they now offer food on site. I hear nothing, but good things about Eaton Street Seafood and plan on returning here soon. It's a couple of blocks from the Historic Key West Seaport. Cool art deco exterior with superb seafood on the inside.

Brew Pub

WATERFRONT BREWERY
This new hangout on the Key West waterfront combines two popular interests, seafood and beer. They don't just serve seafood. Their menu is diverse and has something for everyone. They also brew at least a dozen different beers at any given time and stock many others. Their claim to fame besides being the new star on the marina, was that Zac Brown did a small popup show here last year at the Brewery.

Key Lime Pie

KERMIT'S KEY LIME PIE SHOPPE
Most days of the week if you pass by this Elizabeth Street sweets shop you'll find a guy dressed head to toe in lime green chef's attire including his hat and shoes. This is none other than Kermit himself who greets customers, pie in hand, and beckons them in to try his wares. Some of the best desserts in town can be found here. My favorite thing to get at Kermit's is his chocolate covered Key Lime pie on a stick. It's very rich and delicious and is a must try.

BLUE HEAVEN
Blue Heaven's version of Key Lime pie includes a traditional recipe made with real Key Lime juice plus a topping of mile high meringue. This quirky little restaurant found in the Bahama Village section of Key West occupies the spot formerly known to be Ernest Hemingway's boxing ring. When his wife built a pool in his backyard, he moved his boxing ring to this location.

PEPE'S

Great slice of tart, just like I like it, this Key Lime pie is served with whipped cream on top. This is reputed to be Key West's oldest eating house started in 1909. Also excellent graham cracker crust on this made by hand dessert.

SCOOTERS

SUNSHINE SCOOTERS

This is my go to rental when I hit town. We usually park the rental car that we got in Miami and trade it for two wheeled transportation. It makes it a heck of a lot easier to get around and park in Old Town Key West and also allows you to enjoy the fragrances of nature and the warm sunshine. Sunshine Scooters has really good rates and new equipment. If you're a first time rider or even a little shaky they won't send you out until you're both comfortable with your abilities.

My wife knows that a scooter is the best way to get around in Key West, especially when it comes to finding a parking space.

One of the best sunrises I have ever seen. Captured on Stock Island. Photo by Stacy Lee.

A life-sized Marilyn Monroe outside the Tropic Cinema. Photo by Mark Lee.

This is Hemingway's bed. The headboard was actually made from a gate found on his travels. The hinge pins can still be seen on the left side. Photo by Mark Lee

One of the famous six toed Hemingway cats naps on top of a case containing some of his books and belongings. Photo by Mark Lee.

This fountain is actually made from a urinal that Hemingway dragged home from Sloppy Joes Bar. Look closely at the bottom and you can see that it has been decorated by Spanish tile to dress it up a bit. Photo by Mark Lee.

ACKNOWLEDGEMENTS

First, I want to thank my daughter Maddy for taking my photo for the back cover of the book. She also took the picture for my first book and she's never let me forget that the fact that I forgot to give her credit. I also want to thank some of my new friends that have helped me along the way in putting this book together: Tom Corcoran, Winnie DeMent, Chris and Noelle Itrato, David Thibault, Key West Chris Rehm and Captain Marlin Scott and his wife Diane. When I'm not in Key West I keep up with what's going on by listening to Captain Scott's daily Fish Monster Report on Facebook. I've come to rely on him for his excellent color commentary of the goings on in my favorite island nation. My thanks also goes out to my good friend David Sloan who has always been willing to help me along the way and it's much appreciated.

Of course I could not have done all of this without the love and support of my family and my favorite travel partner, my wife Stacye. We've had many travel adventures and I'm looking forward to many more. If I've left anyone out I apologize and I'll be sure to mention you in the next book. Just ask Maddy.

To contact me with questions, comments, or request autographed copies of this book:
Email: keylimepress@gmail.com

ABOUT THE AUTHOR

Mark Lee's first book, *The Ultimate Key West Guide*, debuted as the #1 Florida Keys Travel Guide on Amazon.com in May 2015. Since then he has spent his spare time traveling up and down the Florida Keys checking out new places to eat and drink just for you! Hey, somebody's got to do it.

Mark does have a real job but when he's not working in the medical field he enjoys kicking back on a beach with his wife and soaking up the sun with the sounds of waves in the background.

Made in United States
North Haven, CT
07 April 2022

18001109R00133